Praise for
It's Better to Be Ove...
Than Under ...

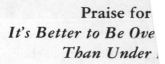

"In this book, filled with laughter and wisdom, Eda LeShan grips our attention and quite spontaneously makes us see what we have failed to see as we face the boundaries of the new country of old age. She does it in her inimitable way of describing her own stumbles and amazements, her own fears and determination. She takes us in and suddenly we recognize where we are, and become fascinated by her insights and our own new ones. This book opens the door to much we have feared or wished to shut out, and lets in lots of sunshine."

—MAY SARTON

"LeShan's style is outspoken, funny and personal. She offers readers plenty of advice on growing older, if not gracefully, at least without fear and regret."

—*AARP Bulletin*

"Good for Eda LeShan who's old enough to write about age and young enough to celebrate with joy."

—LOIS WYSE

"With flat-out honesty and directness, LeShan draws from her experience as a mother, wife, and working woman, (and) has written a book that is by turns hilarious, sharply observant, moving and inspiring. It's a book that speaks to anyone who is getting older, which, if you think a second, means everybody."

—*Book Page* (Nashville, TN)

IT'S BETTER TO BE OVER THE HILL THAN UNDER IT

Thoughts on Life Over Sixty

Eda LeShan

Newmarket Press
Newmarket Press
New York

FOR LARRY:
Forty-six years is not enough.
Grow old along with me
or you're in big trouble!

---

91 92 93 94   10 9 8 7 6 5 4 3 2 1

Library of Congress Cataloging-in-Publication Data

LeShan, Eda J.
It's better to be over the hill than under it : thoughts on life over sixty / Eda LeShan.
p.   cm.
Essays originally published in syndicated columns.
ISBN 1-55704-102-4
1. Old age—United States.   2. Aged—United States—Psychology.   I. Title.
HQ1064.U5L468   1990
305.26'0973—dc20   90-41274
                                                              CIP

Quantity Purchases
Companies, professional groups, clubs, and other organizations may qualify for special terms when ordering quantities of this title. For information, write Special Sales, Newmarket Press, 18 East 48th Street, New York, N.Y. 10017, or call (212) 832-3575.

Manufactured in the United States of America

First Paperback Edition

CONTENTS

Foreword *ix*

Introduction 3

I
LOVING AND LIVING

Thanksgiving Thoughts 9

The Week I Lost Thursday *11*

Beating the Holiday Blues *15*

The Dr. Ruth Syndrome *18*

Be Kind to Your Brain—It Has a Mind of Its
 Own *21*

The Only Thing I Understand About Computers
 Is "Overload" *23*

Getting Angry at Getting Old—Why Not? *26*

Children Deprived of Living Grandparents *29*

Reluctant Grandparents *32*

Handmade Gifts *35*

When Our Children or Grandchildren
 Bring Home Strangers *38*

When You Learn a Grandchild Is Gay *42*

Is It Our Money or Theirs? *45*

When Sisters Live Together *48*

I Remain Shamelessly Romantic *51*

Dealing With Anger *54*

Divorce After Sixty *57*

When Our Children Divorce *60*

Facing Up to a Friend's Illness *63*

An Open Letter to the Tooth Fairy   66
What Can Be Done About Aged-Parent Abuse   69
The Death of an Adult Child   73
Keeping Connected to Young People   77
Progress Sometimes Drives Me Crazy   79
Different Ways of Dealing With a Serious Illness 81
Some Mental Exercises When Depression Hits   84
If You Dare to Die Before Me, I'll Kill You!   87
When You're Alone on a Holiday   90
Silence Can Be Golden   93
The Season to Celebrate Children   96
Nothing Is Simple Anymore   99

II
MEMORIES

A Feeling of Surprise   105
For All Those Born Before 1930   107
Find Yourself a Carousel   109
Necessary Pilgrimages   112
We Raised Ambassadors of Freedom   115
Our Personal Ghosts   118
My Mother's Tree   121
Telling It Like It Was   124
The Many Faces of Friendship   128
When Relationships End   130
Old Friendships   133
Remembering Loved Ones   135
The Circle of Caring   137
Happy *Old* Years   140

III
GROWING AND CHANGING

Taking Risks   145

The Health Cult   148
Saving and Spending   150
The Dead Weight of Big Lies   153
One Person Makes a Difference   156
How to Survive the News   159
Plant a Tree   162
A New Life—As a Volunteer   164
Our Assets in the Job Market   166
The *No*-Retirement Blues   169
Will I Ever Know Who "Deep Throat" Is?   172
We Are Not Our Children's Children   175
Dealing With the Retirement Blues   178
Things You Can Do Sitting Down   181
On Being an Older Grandparent   184
Are You Playing Regularly?   186
The Power of Pets   189
Picture Buttons   192
Keep Moving!   195
When Children and Grandchildren Seek
    Psychotherapy   197
When It Becomes a Matter of Changing—
    or Dying   200
A Living Will   203
Facing Up to Our Mortality   205
The Brain: Use It or Lose It   208
How to Be a Better Grandparent   211
Don't Wait!   214
The Secret of a Happy Holiday   216
Children—Our Most Precious Gifts   219
The Shock of Changing Roles   222
The Passion That Can Last Forever: Growing   225

Some New Thoughts on
"Over the Hill"

For almost three years in my weekly columns in *Newsday* I have been exhorting my readers to always remember that life is fluid, not static, at any stage of living. So why am I surprised to have to confront what has happened to me since this book was first published in hardcover? It's difficult to always live up to one's own philosophy! Despite what I think and write about the necessity to keep growing and changing all the days of our lives, I am shocked at all that has happened to me.

But the more I think about it, and despite my surprise, I have managed to use my major crisis of this past year for growing. This was a stroke in December of 1990. Eight months later, as I write this addendum, I am doing well physically despite a few annoying reminders of the event (weak left arm, numb fingers, my brain turning to Jell-O in the presence of too many people and too much noise) but I was very, very lucky. The stroke was on the right side of my brain, both literally and figuratively; it never interfered with speech and typing came back in about a month—so my identity is intact.

I think I have gone through all the to-be-expected psychological stages. Denial at first—when my left leg seemed to have stopped working, I figured I'd see a doctor after some workmen had finished installing new windows in my apartment house. Fortunately my daughter called and said, "Mom, you have to decide between the windows and your life." I did. After a month or two I realized I hadn't really faced being terrified by this crisis. I began to have dreams of terror and rage; how dare my body have threatened me with my mortality. When awful nightmares started, I resorted promptly to the method by which I have dealt with crises for over thirty years—I went back into therapy. My best way of growing beyond trauma is to find a wise companion for new explorations into my unconscious. What I found—and continue to study—is that any serious illness, chronic disorder, or disability forces us to reassess our lives and our eventual death. I have to face the fact that I had ignored my physical self as if I could go on abusing it (wrong diet, not enough exercise, terrible overwork and stress), as if I were still a kid and could get away with it. I have stopped being so angry (depression is also part of a stroke) and am trying hard to change much of my former lifestyle.

I write about this at length because it has been the major change. I also have found myself more aware of aging and ordinary illnesses and new vulnerabilities. I see my dentist, my eye doctor, my family physician, and my therapist far more often. My friends and I discuss our health problems just as out mothers used to do, which drove us crazy and we never understood. More friends and relatives have died—bereavement inevitably becomes an integral part of life if we survive. About two percent of the mail I receive tells me that I am a worrywart and that one can be perfectly healthy and happy in old age. Ninety-eight percent of the mail is on the theme "Thank God someone is saying it like is!" But while I surely do focus a lot of attention on the difficult challenges of aging, I try to maintain some humor and optimism, even though the world around us offers little cause for serenity and joy. I didn't think that in my latest years I would feel such grief—wars, cities brought to their metaphorical knees, homelessness, unemployment, the spending of trillions on weapons of war when we have fewer enemies all the time, a wave of greed and immorality, a drug epidemic, and a sense of hopeless despair among the young. We hoped to leave the world better than we found it. I tell my aching soul, "Forget it!" But I still put up a fight wherever I can.

A recent *Newsday* column of mine called "One Impossible Loss" discussed how, with both the joys and sorrows of life, there is really only one truly fatal loss and that is when we lose ourselves. We feel devastated when we are alone with this only companion we have from birth to death. A friend says, "I will have to make the trip alone so I know it will be boring and horrible." I want to ask her where will *she* be— is there any hope of friendship and solace from that quarter? Losing oneself is also giving too much to others and forgetting one's own needs. Do we take the time to nurture and love ourselves? I'm convinced that among several reasons for my own illness was that I was taking care of everyone else's needs and demands and not my own.

When we lose the companionship of that inner self that depends entirely on our good graces, then depression, illness, anger, and a terrible loneliness may well be the price we pay.

So nothing truly basic has changed beyond external experiences. All they have done is to confirm that old age requires humor, courage, a willingness to search within, and a never-ending capacity to go on making our lives as meaningful as possible.

Eda LeShan
August 1991

INTRODUCTION
Looking Forward

Strange things began to happen to me somewhere between my sixtieth and sixty-second birthday. I got dizzy if my husband, Larry, pushed me on a swing in Central Park. After years of riding a bike all around Long Beach Island, New Jersey, and up hill and down dale on Cape Cod, suddenly, one day, I was frightened—afraid I'd fall off. Painting a porch I had painted every other year for several years, this time I ended up with a sacroiliac that crippled me for months. I also began to notice that even if I stayed on a maintenance diet that had worked for about six years, I now began gaining weight. And, of course, I would rush madly about the house searching for my reading glasses when they were hanging around my neck.

There was no doubt about it: all my clever psychological techniques of denial weren't working anymore; I was getting old. My reaction to this awful truth was very simple: I would write a nostalgic book, a plaintive appeal. It would be entitled *Oh, To Be Fifty Again*. The final blow which set me at the crossroads between a major depression and writing a book was an event that occurred in 1980 at the fortieth reunion of my high-school class. There I met a classmate I hadn't seen

since our graduation in 1940. We had a lovely time together—I was sorry we hadn't kept in touch—and when the
party ended, I said, "Gee, Estelle, I hope it won't be another
forty years." Estelle replied quite unkindly, I thought, "Eda,
it *can't* be!" That did it. Not only physical limitations and
mental fogginess, but *mortality* itself; what a blow.

So I wrote the book; I faced being in my sixties. People
often asked me, after the book was published, if there would
be sequels *Oh, To Be Seventy Again* and *Oh, To Be Eighty
Again*. It seemed very unlikely, but at that time it never
occurred to me what a dumb idea that would be.

When *Oh, To Be Fifty Again* was published, I was interviewed by a lovely reporter from *Newsday*, Betty Ommer-
man. She was a good interviewer and I poured out my heart
about how I felt about getting old. A few weeks later a *Newsday* editor, now my guardian angel, Barbara Schuler, called
and asked me if I'd ever thought of writing a regular column
on getting old. For a moment I felt insulted and panic-
stricken. I still inwardly perceived of myself as a thirty-
five-year-old child psychologist and parent and family-life
educator. I was smart as hell about children but what did I
know about old age?

But nobody was offering me a column on childraising and
somewhat reluctantly I began a very slow process of revising
my self-image. Along the course of this difficult process, my
agent called me one day and said there was a producer in
Hollywood who was trying to develop a television show in
which there would be a panel of experts in different fields
and an audience that could ask questions. "Oh, wonderful!"
I exclaimed, "I'll be able to talk about children again!" "No,
Eda," she said—another Estelle in my life. "They want you
to talk about getting old." The final blow to my old self-
image—the beginning of awareness. What I didn't know, as
I started writing a column, "Life Over Sixty," every Saturday

in *Newsday*, was that this was also the beginning of the most important emotional adjustment to the final stage in my life: ACCEPTANCE. Now, as I look back over all the columns I have written in *Newsday* I realize that no matter what the specific subject, I was always wrestling with the developmental stage appropriate to my time of life. No more books "Oh To Be" something else, some other age. There is no turning back. Here I am, and every day I am getting older and I cannot turn the clock back. But what I began to realize through my column was that despite advancing years *I was not helpless*. And neither were any of my readers, no matter what their age, their disabilities, their crises, hardships, and challenges.

I was really not consciously aware of what was happening to me until I had been writing the column for about two years. I must be a slow learner! Because in the first place I was getting the most wonderful and plentiful letters from readers who wanted to share their lives with mine, and after a while I began noticing that as I finished each column, there were a few duds, a few merely adequate, but in general, having written more than twenty books, *I felt I was writing better than I had ever written before*. Writing the column finally taught me that looking backward is for cowards; the real test was: Could I deal creatively with the present, no matter what the inevitable aspects of aging were, and could I anticipate each day ahead?

This book is about my arrival at *acceptance*. It is about who we are and where we are right now; it is an acceptance of the future, despite its increasing limitations. It is a belief in new opportunities. How did I know, wishing to be fifty again, that I would do my best writing in my mid- and late sixties?

No matter how old I am allowed to get, there will be surprises all the time. I meet someone at a conference and within ten minutes we know we will be friends for as long as we live. I see a sunset like none other I have ever seen before. My husband, Larry, gives the most brilliant speech I have ever heard him give. I find a new place with a marvelous view in which to work. I get an invitation, after all, to give a speech on childraising!

I hope I'll still be alive when we stop making weapons and make war on poverty instead. I hope I'll live long enough to see pleasure driving limited in major cities. I hope we will become color blind—maybe, although it is surely touch and go, I might live to see the end of apartheid. Is it possible I will live long enough for there to be electric commuter trains, and major highways turned into housing projects? Who knows?

I will probably live to see my grandchild graduate from high school, if I'm lucky, but if I live that long, there will also be anguish and unbelievable pain at the loss of people I love.

But my focus is on the future, nevertheless, not on the past. We are alive and it's better than being dead. I now settle for that rather than wishing to go back to an earlier time.

And the message I learned and which I try to communicate in all these columns is that it is good to be alive so long as we know who we are, accept where we are, and can still bring meaning into our lives by our own creativity and what we can do for others. I am not so crazy as to be so accepting of aging that I might write a book called *Oh, To Be Ninety, At Last!* but I have learned to accept exactly where I am, and I hope others will join me in holding on to precious memories, but at the same time wondering how we can use today and tomorrow for the utmost fulfillment of which we are capable.

I

LOVING
AND
LIVING

"Love is the most important ingredient in living, children are our greatest treasure, all human beings all over the world need and deserve the same opportunities for the fullest use of their abilities, and this planet, the only one we know, must be treasured and not defiled."

Thanksgiving Thoughts

FOR THOSE OF US OVER SIXTY, HIGH ON THE LIST OF gratitude should be that we are still alive! Even if it hurts! Even if we feel thirty-five inside of our heads and can no longer even count the wrinkles. Even if that bald-headed fellow is the one we fell in love with because he had gorgeous red hair; even if that sexy girl in the bathing suit you married fifty years ago now tips the scale at two hundred. Even if rain makes us hurt and we get out of breath dialing a telephone. Even if the doctor says it's cataract time or prostate time.

What I hope is that you feel thankful to be alive because you still feel like a person, no matter what the changes. At any age there is only one reason to be thankful to be alive and that is that you love your closest companion—yourself; and you know who you are and you are glad to be who you are.

Being thankful to be alive takes hard work. It means that no matter what your physical handicaps may be you are still the kind of person who can do something mean-ingful for somebody else. If your legs don't work and you're in a wheelchair, you can still hold someone's hand when he or she is sad; you can still smile at, even kiss, a nurse who is tired and whose feet hurt and yet who is working on Thanksgiving because of your needs.

What makes us glad to be alive is if there is nothing we hate about ourselves, nothing for which we cannot forgive ourselves. I know a doctor who feels guilty and angry because he feels he chose the wrong profession; he became a doctor and sooner or later many of his patients died, so he hates himself for not picking an easier profession! Imagine! Guilt for being a caring person! If there are things in our lives that we wish we had not done or things we wish we had done, we can make amends so long as there is breath left in our bodies. I knew a man who had never gone to Florence, Italy, but had longed to see the works of Michelangelo, and went two months before he died of cancer. No business left unfinished. I know a woman in a hospital who asked the nurse for a straw and some olives. The nurse thought she was hallucinating, but she got them. The woman called a sister she hadn't spoken to for ten years and asked her to come to the hospital—where she handed her an "olive branch"!

On this best of all American holidays, when we are joined together as one family, let us give thanks we are still alive and can still give understanding and love to others.

The Week
I Lost Thursday

I T WAS A VERY BUSY WEEK—LOTS OF CHORES TO TAKE care of, an article to type, preparations for the visit of my daughter and granddaughter. I made up my mind I'd have to get up very early in order to get everything done before they arrived. I went shopping at the su permarket, and I found a plumbing supply company where I could get a new stopper for the bathtub, and I bought myself a short summer bathrobe, and I found three books to give to my granddaughter that I thought she'd like. I made up a package of things to take to my father's house when we went to see him on Saturday— I ran around all day and accomplished a lot, very efficiently.

And then I went home to wait for my daughter and granddaughter to come. I figured with Friday traffic, they might arrive quite late. When my husband came home for supper he said, "I've been trying to reach you all day, but you were out. You got me all confused; today isn't Friday, it's Thursday."

I was so well organized that I had done all the things

I was supposed to do on Friday, but I had missed all my
Thursday appointments—the dentist, the hairdresser,
and delivering a manuscript to my agent.

I was devastated. This was something I had never done
before in my whole life. I have always been well organized; in more than forty-five years I had never missed
a professional obligation even though my schedule of
speaking engagements was always very complicated. In
my whole life I had never missed an appointment.

My immediate reaction was, this is the early-warning
sign of senility—or worse. It's all downhill to the cem-
etery from now on; all the vitamins and minerals my
daughter has instructed me to take aren't working—my
mind is going. I was scared to death. Is there anyone
over sixty who hasn't shared at least a moment or two
of such anxiety?

I was at a crossroads—two possible choices—and I
think I made the right decision. The choice I rejected
was to go on assuming that old age was upon me and
that I had become mentally incompetent. The choice I
decided upon was to see if I could figure out what other
alternative reasons there might be for my having lost
Thursday.

It really wasn't that hard to figure out. I was unusually
tired that week; I had been trying to do much more
than anyone of *any* age could comfortably handle. Too
many demands were being made on me by other people
and I had allowed that to happen. The serenity and
tranquility I need at least some of the time to feel good,
had been set aside too long. I'd been stuck in the city,
with its brick walls and noise and crowds, too long and

was starving for a day in the country. And probably most of all, I was feeling ambivalent about my daughter's visit. In order to hide my unconscious feelings, I turned Thursday into Friday to prove to myself how eager I was for her arrival. On the one hand I adore both my daughter and my granddaughter, and don't get a chance to see them very often. On the other hand, feeling so exhausted beforehand, the thought of the usual catastrophic changes that would take place in my living room, with the sleeping bags and suitcases, and the number of towels that would be lying wet all over the bathroom, and my darling granddaughter's energy level from six in the morning to bedtime—I finally faced it: I wasn't one hundred percent thrilled, as I felt I should be.

What I finally realized, even halfway through this exercise in introspection, is that if I'd been forty and lost a Thursday, I would have known more quickly the roles of fatigue and mixed feelings. At sixty-five, my first reaction had been terror that I was losing my marbles. It behooves all of us who can no longer fall into the "spring chicken" category to watch out for such misjudgments. Far be it from me to suggest that aging doesn't bring with it some physiological changes, but it is also true that many of us jump to the wrong conclusions about ourselves because we are looking at the calendar too often and are not examining our environment, our feelings, the circumstances of our lives, often enough.

Before we conclude that the mind is failing, we need to have a long, serious, honest talk with ourselves. Most of the time the issue is not our age but the fact that we are allowing ourselves to be exploited by other people's needs and are not being as loving as we need to be toward ourselves.

P.S. Once I faced my ambivalent feelings, I had a fine time with my daughter and my gorgeous granddaughter, and gave myself a day's rest in bed when they went home. And I knew it was Monday.

Beating the Holiday Blues

WERE YOU ALONE DURING CHANUKAH, OR ARE YOU going to be alone for Christmas? Are you widowed and do the children and grandchildren live too far away, or is this the year they visit the other grandparents? Are you single and your closest friend has gone to Florida? Well, I'm here to tell you being alone doesn't have to be the end of the world.

A certain amount of self-pity is allowable; have a good cry, feel real sorry for yourself—and then get busy.

First of all, buy yourself some flowers or winter decorations and give yourself a pleasing environment. Then make up your mind what terrific gift you can give yourself. It doesn't have to cost much; maybe you're such a cheapskate that you haven't bought yourself a new can opener; this is the moment. Or maybe, being properly health-conscious, the gift you need badly is a hot dog from the umbrella cart on the corner—a special treat. Or even more likely, allow yourself the extravagance of calling someone you love.

The second assignment is to try to think of someone who is worse off than you are: your next-door neighbor, who hasn't any grandchildren, even far away, and whose daughter died at twenty-eight a year ago; or your cousin, just recently widowed, living alone for the first time in his life and trying to be so brave; or the three children in a foster home down the block, whose mother is in prison and whose father is a drug addict. Invite the neighbor or the cousin, or both, to have a simple dinner with you; invite the children over for afternoon tea with presents. I have a friend who spends every Christmas day at a Salvation Army headquarters serving turkey dinners and says, "I feel so good about myself and I know it means a lot to the people I talk to, and I come home so tired, I haven't got the time or energy to feel sorry for myself."

When we cannot bear to be alone, it means we do not properly value or appreciate the only companion we will have from birth to death—ourselves. Of course, we mourn for people we loved who are gone; of course, memories of holidays past, with a family all together, are painful. (We forget it wasn't all bliss, but that's okay. If good memories make us sad, they tell us how lucky we are to have them.) I believe in genuine grief and the need for its expression but hopefully it can eventually lead us back into life and a renewed sense of our own powers, our own lovability. No matter how many people may have loved us during our lives, the love we need most of all is the love we can give ourselves. It's the springboard to a creative and meaningful and fulfilling life when we are alone.

You will find that when you have given yourself the gifts of beauty and friendship and service to others, you will be ready to not only *sound* happy, but *be* happy when the grandchildren or an old friend or a son or daughter calls on the holiday evening and says, "Where have you been? I've been trying to reach you all day." If you can say, "I've been *living*," you will have beaten the holiday blues.

The Dr. Ruth Syndrome

I HAVE TO GET MIGHTY CLOSE TO ANY OLDER MAN or woman if I want to find out about their sex lives! It is my conclusion that this would not be true if everyone over sixty were having a rollicking good time. The reason nobody's talking is because of a new kind of guilt that is driving us crazy.

The reasons we are ricocheting from wall to wall is that when we were young, we felt guilty about being sexual—sometimes even after our parents had gotten us safely married and could breathe a sigh of relief. (I was twenty-two when I got married and my mother was noticeably relieved.) It was beginning to be okay for women, in particular, to enjoy sex—the marriage manuals of the 1940s exhorted the menfolk to play gently on us as if we were delicate violins!—but we weren't exactly boasting in public about our pleasures. There was a lot of guilt about being too sexy in those ancient times.

And here we are now, told by Dr. Ruth and an assortment of other manic people that our hormones are not declining, it's all in our heads, and there is no reason why we shouldn't be gleefully rolling in the hay at least twice a week. It's just about impossible to get any man on Social Security to admit the gonads are quieting down, but I'm here to tell you that if you get a group of ladies into the right state of relaxation, they will guiltily giggle the truth: they are really into hugging and cuddling more than you-know-what. One sixty-two-year-old told me, "I feel as if there's something wrong with me, but I almost never think about sex anymore. No more powerful urges, no more fantasies—my idea of heaven is a really hot game of bridge followed by a mushroom pizza." Another woman, seduced into truthfulness, said, "I got into a really intimate conversation with my thirty-nine-year-old daughter, who is very happily married, and who said even she's down to about twice a month! I felt so relieved!"

Frankly, I deeply resent the show-biz approach to the private lives each of us has a right to, and having started my adult life feeling guilty about too much sex I'll be damned if I'll end my days feeling guilty about too little sex. I'm not going to keep any records and I'm not going to read about any more joys and I'm not going to have any sex games on my coffee table. The truth is that there is an army of us senior-types who know we are real men and real women in a hundred different avenues of our lives, even if we never tried fifty-seven varieties of positions.

There is, of course, another truth sometimes (if not always!) overlooked by the expert who assures us sex can still be great at ninety-five. I'm sure he or she is right for a few remarkable people, and that's terrific, but by sixty-five or seventy a great many of us are widowed and don't feel inclined to seek another partner. A friend of mine says, "Listen, I've been living alone for ten years and I'm still waiting for some doctor to talk about how great it is to have a teddy bear to cuddle in bed!"

It might be a source of relief if we kept a record of who is writing articles and books or appearing on TV, exhorting us to a never-ending orgasmic life. Most of them are much younger than we are!

Be Kind
to Your Brain—
It Has a Mind of Its Own

I JUST WALKED FROM MY BEDROOM INTO MY OFFICE. I then walked back into the bedroom because of course I'd forgotten the purpose of my trip. The television was on in the bedroom, showing some really old movie, and I noticed a woman on the screen. "Oh, that's Louise Fazenda," I said to myself, and then tried to figure out what I was doing and why. And then came this wild double take: LOUISE FAZENDA?!?! Why, in the name of all the mysteries of the human mind, had I remembered a name of such total insignificance (to me, not her) in the movies of the twenties and thirties?

Where, in what strange pocket of my brain, what mad synapses, had that come from when I sometimes forget the names of close friends, can never find my glasses (even when around my neck), and live more and more in a world where I have to just wait and see what will surface in its own good time when I'm trying to remember something? In sixty-seven years of remembering,

Louise Fazenda's name had never been on any list of my priorities.

I never did get back to why I went into my office, but having now returned to it, I am reflecting on this very strange and awesome brain of mine. The longer I live the more it seems to have a life of its own. I always thought my brain belonged to me—was my servant, as it were. Now I find that it has its own priorities, eccentricities, and schedules. I have two choices: I can fight it, knowing I can't win, or I can go along for the ride, wherever it may take me.

Maybe today it was more important to my brain to think back nostalgically about the movies of my childhood. Maybe when I first heard the name "Fazenda," it had an unusually lyrical sound. Maybe in some movie she reminded me of my aunt Lilly, who was fey and delightful, and whom I adored and who looked a little like her. Maybe there is some movie theme that knocked me out for some unconscious reason. It doesn't seem to matter. I feel calm and happy, and to tell you the truth, I no longer care what I was trying to remember. If I need it, it will come back after I've taken a few extra vitamins. Maybe my brain was saying, "Take a rest."

I hate computers with a passion, but the one above my neck fascinates me. It is always so full of surprises. Somewhere inside there must have been software on Louise Fazenda. How did it get there? For the sake of surviving in the midst of general internal and external chaos, I am going to assume my brain is my friend. What choice do I have?

The Only Thing
I Understand About
Computers Is "Overload"

Up until quite recently, if anyone suggested I should get a computer, I immediately ran for a yellow pad and a pencil to assert my right to remain rigid and inflexible in my attitude toward any kind of electrical equipment. I figured that my adjustment to the toaster and the telephone and the television was quite enough for one lifetime. But now I have a new feeling of compassion for computers.

One day, while I was waiting at the gate for my seat assignment at an airport, the woman at the desk told me there would be a delay. "The computer is down," she said. I asked her what that meant, exactly, and she said, "It's because of overload."

A wave of sympathy and understanding came over me. How do you like that, I thought to myself, computers have something in common with old people like me!

There is one anxiety about aging that I think we could well do without, and that is when we can't remember a

name, or can't recall what it is we have started to do, or
forget a telephone number we have known for twenty
years. It does not, automatically, mean we are getting
senile. What it does mean is that we are in a state of
overload.

Think for a minute about the facts our brains have
had to absorb since the day we were born: not to cross
a street if the light is red; how to make a lamb stew;
how to drive a car; the multiplication table (I still haven't
fully mastered that, I'm sorry to say). If we tried to list
all the facts we have had to learn, the skills, the things
we have had to remember, it would probably take several years to complete the list.

Next time I can't remember my own telephone number, I will just assume that my brain is "in a down mode"
due to "overload." And what I will assume happens, I
believe, to be the truth.

The older we get the more information we have to
discard in order to remember Important Things. I see
a woman in the lobby of a theater, and I cannot remember her name. But I do remember how kind she was to
my daughter when we were neighbors, and I remember
how devastated she was when her dog was run over and
I remember that she had a terrible allergy to roses. I
can recall the important human things I know about her,
and her name seems irrelevant as I recall the quality of
her personality.

While I may not know as many facts as I once did, I
remember love and good deeds and the uniqueness of
each person. I may forget everything I meant to buy at
the supermarket, because of course I left my list at
home, but I am learning the names of birds who come

to my feeder, and I never forget to have food ready when the ducks and geese bring their children around in the spring. I am remembering more of the things that are important and relevant to the experiences of growing older, and forgetting things that seem quite trivial at this time of my life.

A certain kind of forgetting is a necessary developmental task of getting old. What we are doing is coming closer to the meditative state that might well make our deaths easier to face. We are steadily moving from the world of *Doing* to the world of *Being*. We want to feel that we are part of nature and that nature is a part of us—that there is a larger universe beyond the traffic, the noise, the stress and strain of our daily lives. We are in search of serenity. Overload is out, tranquility is in; that is a necessary requirement for growing older gracefully.

It is natural for us to be afraid of our increasing forgetfulness, because senility and Alzheimer's disease are realities of life. But the majority of us are in a state of overload, and what we need to start to do is become consciously selective about how we can relieve our poor, tired, overloaded brains. When we worry about what we are forgetting, it is in large part because the process has been unconscious—we don't feel we are in control. The minute we begin to tell ourselves we can choose what to forget, we will feel more autonomous. Chances are we will probably become less boring to others, too, as we discard the garbage in our heads—the stuff we just don't need anymore—and become more choosy and more contemplative. Just don't forget about not crossing at red lights!

Getting Angry
at Getting Old—
Why Not?

I'M LYING IN BED, SEE, AND IT'S TWO O'CLOCK IN THE morning. I figure it's going to rain or snow because my arthritic feet hurt so much. There's a finger on my left hand that also hurts like the very devil for the same reason. I have a toothache too—my dentist has told me that it takes at least three times as long to get over an infection now than when I was young. To keep from going crazy, I'm listening to the radio—"The Larry King Show," and his guest is David Brown, film producer (*Jaws, Cocoon,* etc.) and husband of Helen Gurley Brown. He's seventy-one and he's written a book about getting old. I hear him say (no kidding!), "There is absolutely no reason you can't feel as well as you did at fifty, and the secret is never to stop working." I want to kill him!

At fifty I could ride a bicycle ten miles a day. At fifty I almost never needed a prescription drug. No aches or pains, no getting tired by four in the afternoon, no elderly parents to worry about. Sixty-seven is *not* the same by any stretch of the imagination.

I think of the mail I receive; a very small proportion of those who write to me are in perfect health and have enough money to be comfortable, and are in a position to go on working at some job they love, as Mr. Brown is fortunate enough to be doing. Lucky people, with terrific genes for good health, who, like Mr. Brown, are able to be very active, without money worries. They are few and far between.

The majority of people from about sixty-five on up are not so lucky. I wonder how many others were silently, bitterly laughing with me at two A.M. But I don't worry about the people who got angry like me. I worry about the people who have been trying terribly hard to deny the fact of old age and can have this denial reinforced by people who are so gung ho about getting old.

I worry about the people who are ashamed of their aches and pains, and feel that no one will love them if they ever mention how they feel. I worry about those who have been the victims of forced retirement and feel so useless, who seem to lose their identity, but try to pretend everything is just wonderful and they really would rather play golf four times a week, or live in a crowded trailer park because they can barely stay alive on Social Security. I worry about the old people forced by circumstances to live with their children, who desperately miss the freedom of earlier days and hate being a burden to the younger generation, but who never complain or talk about their feelings.

I wonder if the woman who wrote me this letter was

listening to Larry King on that same night: "I have become permanently crippled and now live with my son,
my daughter-in-law, and my grandson, who has been
forced to share his room with me. I was always an active,
independent person. I only wish I would die so that this
good family that I love could be rid of me and I of this
body I cannot endure."

It is wonderful to be rich and healthy and enjoying
one's life; that is not the lot of most of us, most of the
time. I felt better that morning because I'd gotten so
angry that night. It helps to let oneself feel the feelings
that come—the totally unexpected anger and despair
that so frequently are a part of old age, the psychological,
physical, and financial wounds that present such a challenge just at a time when we may be too worn out to
fight back, deal with the challenges.

For most of us old age is *not* all fun and games. Sto-
icism, silence, and pretending only make life harder. A
good yell once in a while is good for the circulation—
and heaven knows we need as much of that as we can
get.

Children Deprived
of Living Grandparents

I MET AN OLD FRIEND I HADN'T SEEN FOR ABOUT five years. She told me, "I'm a grandmother but I have never seen my granddaugher. She's three and I'm the only living grandparent, and I could give her so much love! It tortures me!"

Of course I was sorry for Connie but I must confess that my first concern was that deprived little child. Unfortunately there are too many young parents who think their anger, their conflicts, or their feelings of having been wronged somewhere along the line are far more important than the fact that children without grandparents are seriously deprived of a kind of emotional nourishment they cannot get from anyone else.

There are, of course, exceptions to this general rule. An adult parent who was abused as a child has every right to protect his or her child from a grandparent who is emotionally disturbed. And, of course, there are families who live thousands of miles apart or whose grandparents have all died—something more and more rare as life expectancy increases.

But the problem I want to address is where grand-children are withheld from grandparents for reasons that have nothing to do with the needs of children.

Connie had a lot of problems with her son: As a child he deeply resented her divorcing his father (an alcoholic) and never quite forgave her, even after he was old enough to understand. As a teenager, he got into serious trouble on many counts, and his mother mishandled a lot of it. He just wants her out of his life for good. Connie is in no way an evil or dangerous person, and whether or not Peter wants to have a close mother-son relationship has nothing to do with his child.

Children desperately need people who will love them unconditionally, which only grandparents can do. They need a context for living—that human beings are born, they grow up, they grow old, and they die. The conti-nuity of life's pattern is best learned from grandparents. A relationship with a grandchild is also the way children get a sense of connection to their own parents' past and to the generations that came before. My grandchild turns to her grandfather when she wants a funny make-believe story; she turns to me to hear about her great-grand-parents, her grandparents, and what her mother was like as a child. She especially appreciates the ways in which her mother drove me crazy!

In every family—except in the case of truly profound pathology—there were *some* good things in background experiences. Peter, if he is fair at all, would have to acknowledge that his mother worked very hard to sup-port him and that her mistakes were never vicious, just maybe not well-informed; he might even acknowledge that his mother's growing up had been full of events that seriously damaged her life.

But a grandparent is usually a necessary asset not to be thrown aside. Sooner or later children themselves discover their own hunger for a sense of the past and the special love that makes no demands but just IS. We have lots of terribly deprived children these days, without homes, without food, without two parents to raise them. To add any other deprivations makes me mad!

Reluctant Grandparents

I HAVE A YOUNG FRIEND WITH A NEW BABY WHO IS livid with fury (but is really feeling rejected and hurt) because her wealthy parents haven't invited her to visit them at their condo in Hawaii. They go for three or four months every winter. They are in their late sixties.

I understand her hurt feelings, but I am also in sympathy with her parents! There comes a time when parenting and grandparenting are *enough already!* Having a chance to rekindle the romance in an old marriage and soak one's old bones in sunshine, and not have to plan a damn thing all day, is what growing older is all about. It doesn't mean we don't love our families, just that we have given all we've got and it is time for a sabbatical.

I received this letter from a forty-two-year-old mother:

> My parents live in Florida and while they are devoted to each other they are woefully out of touch with my children, although I am a good daughter to them. They did not attend my son's Bar Mitzvah, and they send $10 Chanukah presents when they could easily afford F.A.O. Schwarz! My husband's

parents are worse; they live twenty minutes away and you have to beg them to come to some important event for the children. The children never had overnight visits, never were taken to Disneyland or anywhere else. On the rare occasions we get together, none of the grandparents spend time talking to the children.

I remember how shocked I was with the way my mother-in-law behaved with my child. She never invited her to visit at any time during my daughter's childhood— not once; the only personal thing I can remember is that once, when we visited, she set Wendy's hair! I thought that was remarkable!

Most grandparents are overjoyed to have grandchildren and see this as their own immortality. Many grandparents have greatly missed having little kids around and revel in having new playmates. Most grandparents are like me, I think, full of love but easily tired!

However, parents must face the fact that there can be a number of reasons why some grandparents aren't cut out to play this role very well.

One reason is simply burnout related to childraising and needing to be alone together. Adult children should be glad when parents are still that crazy about each other. Other people see grandchildren as a clear indication that they are getting old and this is unendurable—they prefer to deny the passage of time. Some people had a very hard time raising children in the first place and are, frankly, glad to be free at last.

The worst thing parents can do is to make the grandchildren feel that this is somehow their fault: they should be cuter or more polite or whatever. Children need the truth; they sense it whether you say anything or not. Much better to say some people don't like getting older and you remind them, and some people are tired and children wear them out, and some people just aren't too wonderful with their own or anyone else's children. It may be necessary to face the fact that the parents never felt fully wanted and loved and want it to be different for their children. A mother says, "I never felt my mother really liked me, but I was sure she would melt when she saw my adorable baby." Not necessarily. People who weren't crazy about being parents aren't too likely to have a major personality change as grandparents. Resentment and anger on the part of the adult children, and guilt and defensiveness on the part of grandparents, are of no service to grandchildren.

If we are decent and civilized and understand the needs and the vulnerability of young children, it seems to me we have to make some effort to meet the needs of our grandchildren at least some of the time, limiting ourselves to what we can do, and not feeling guilty about what we can't do.

I think it's just fine to insist on your right to freedom and quiet and rest. But there are other things to consider. Nobody loses so much by losing contact with young people than older people. The child inside each of us dries up and dies. And whatever our age, maturity means making some demands on ourselves. In addition these children *are* your immortality, and one of these days you may regret it if they hardly remember you at all.

Handmade Gifts

STEVIE WAS IN TEARS. HE HAD WANTED TO MAKE A terrific wooden sailboat for his grandfather, but when he finished it he hated it and was crying in frustration because the bow was not a perfect V and the sail hung at a crooked angle. His inner vision of perfection was simply beyond his eight-year-old skills. When his mother tried to reassure him and tell him it was a wonderful boat and Grandpa would be delighted, Stevie wailed, "You only say that because you love me!"

Stevie was right; Grandpa *would* be crazy about the boat because he loved his grandson. But even more, because it was a true gift of love—something Stevie had made himself.

Our grandchildren find it very hard to believe that we *really* like the crooked clay candy dish or the uneven potholders, the homemade cookies that weigh a pound and a half apiece, or the strictly modern art that needs an explanation. In this technological age of stuffed animals that can carry on a conversation, of computers for kids, and of grandma's new microwave, how could they possibly think that the gifts they are able to make

are likely to please us? This is a natural reaction, con-
sidering that we tend to give *them* all sorts of mechanical
wonders—presents their parents can't afford, like ten-
speed bicycles and VCRs.

I don't know about you, but I *love* the things my granddaughter can make herself and I know of only one way
to convince her that the things we make have far more
love in them than anything we can buy. No, that doesn't
mean I might not behave like an old fool and spend far
too much for a baby doll like the one I had when I was
a child (now $65, it must have cost my parents all of
$2). What it means is that even though I am a really
lousy knitter and crocheter, I will make a hat and a scarf
for that doll (I could *never* handle a sweater), and my
granddaughter will know there was more love in that
effort than in paying for the doll. She may not *use* the
hat and scarf, and she may not *be crazy* about my hand-
iwork, but she will be quite certain about the love.

If we want out grandchildren to feel happy and con-
fident about the gifts they give us, we need to do some
cooking and sewing and other handicrafts, even if our
sixty- or seventy-year-old skills don't even match theirs.
The message is more important than the medium.

Another kind of loving is expressed in gifts of oneself.
One grandmother found a note from her grandson which
said, "Dear Granma: My present is that on Christmas
morning I will bring you breakfast in bed and be your
slave all day." Grandma was truly thrilled, despite the
fact that Danny's love was so great he included his pet
frog on the breakfast tray along with the lumpy Wheat-
ena and burnt toast and chewable coffee. Her gift was,

"If you are going to be my slave all day, I order you to accompany me to the Museum of Natural History!" A perfect exchange of gifts, speaking to a tender understanding of each other's needs. The very best of all possible gift-giving, without the stress of shopping or the danger of bankruptcy.

When Our Children
or Grandchildren
Bring Home Strangers

WHEN MY PARENTS WERE YOUNG, ENGAGEMENTS might well last for several years. Sexual abstinence was the expected behavior, and young men were supposed to become financially secure before marriage so that they could take care of their wives, who would, of course, stay home and raise the children. My parents were the exceptions in those days because my mother was a working woman, but even they were engaged for more than a year. By the time most young couples got married, the in-laws on both sides had had a pretty good chance to get to know their child's partner.

How times have changed! Our children usually got married but many of them are now divorced and may either be remarried or have a "live-in partner." Something that was once almost unthinkable has become commonplace. Many of us are ricocheting from wall to wall, trying to adjust and accept but not give up our own most basic and precious values. It isn't easy, and one of the most difficult problems is that we are usually presented with strangers quite abruptly. It happens with our adult children if they divorce and seek new relationships, and heaven knows we already, or will soon, have to face these sudden connections among our grandchildren.

If we refuse to make any concessions to the new ways, we will probably lose touch with the people we love. Some adaptation seems to me to be the only way I was able to fulfill my most basic value that love must never be sacrificed to discomfort or pride or inflexibility, and that we wanted to stay close to our daughter, no matter how different her life might be from our own experience.

One Victorian grandmother (who happened to be my mother!), with a heart condition, walked up five flights of a tenement to have "tea" with her eighteen-year-old granddaughter and her boyfriend, bringing along her granddaughter's favorite cookies, and some dishes and silverware. Her explanation: "I love this child and I won't lose her, no matter what." Nothing could have given her granddaughter a clearer message about Grandma's values.

Instead of being frightened by the strangers who enter our lives or having preconceived notions that these strangers are simply too different and can't possibly be suitable companions, we need to look on this situation as an opportunity and a challenge. My husband and I operated on the belief that any young man our daughter brought home from the age of fourteen on had to have some good qualities or our daughter wouldn't have cared for him. With that attitude—open to the search for goodness—we often got so fond of a particular young man that when he was gone, we missed him more than our daughter did!

How does one do it? A son or daughter or grandchild introduces you to someone he or she may have known for a few weeks, maybe a month, and announces, "This is the person I care for right now." We have several choices. We can make it clear that this is totally unacceptable, and *our* parents must be rolling in their graves. We can say we have now been pushed too far—good heavens, this person is of a different religion or color or even political party! If this child or grandchild wants to see us, THAT PERSON is not to come along. Or, we can say we need a little time and understanding, because our background and life experiences were so different, but we are going to make every effort to make this new person part of our lives.

Acting on the second choice seems to me to be the wiser. It may well be that our relative has actually made a foolish, even a dangerous, choice. Sending the couple packing means we can have no input on how things turn out. By staying very much in touch, without being critical, we make it possible to be present to help this child or grandchild pick up the pieces later on.

Staying close and welcoming a stranger may, on some occasions, be the only way we can help our loved one begin to see that a particular stranger is seriously neurotic or possibly psychopathic or opportunistic. Even someone in love sooner or later recognizes being exploited and hurt.

One grandmother, very concerned about a granddaughter who came to visit with a man twenty years her senior, extolled his virtues, made it clear she trusted her grandchild's judgment, and made this stranger comfortable and at ease in her home. Six months later she got a letter from her granddaughter: "Nana, I hope you won't be too disappointed since I know you liked him, but I decided there were just too many years between us." If Grandma had refused her friendship, chances are her granddaughter might have had to prove she had been right in her choice.

One way to go on feeling young is to have new adventures, and getting to know strangers can be an adventure as well as a way to maintain precious connections.

When You Learn
a Grandchild Is Gay

A GENERATION AGO, FEW PARENTS WERE EVER told directly that a son or daughter was gay. They surely must have come to suspect; there was a whole lot of energy being used up in denial, but nobody talked; life in the closet was well concealed, much to the detriment and unhappiness of many homosexuals and lesbians.

In spite of a slightly more enlightened view in recent years, grandparents are still more than likely to be ricocheting from wall to wall when the news is out. When we were young, nobody ever said a word about the two schoolteachers who had lived together for thirty years or about Uncle Joe, who seemed to want to be a bachelor forever. When we heard anything about homosexuals it was usually that they were depraved or sick or disgusting or promiscuous, or all of these. We, like most of our generation, were ignorant and prejudiced.

Theories about homosexuality were wrong; the impression that homosexuals behaved in antisocial, unacceptable ways was often true, but not for the reasons we were given. Before the closet door began to open, many gay people would have viewed themselves as worthless in some way because this was how they were labeled by society. Feelings of self-hatred lead to self-destructive behavior, whether one is heterosexual or homosexual. Wife beaters or child molesters, hetero-sexual as all get-out, are people who despise themselves. So too homosexuals, discarded by society, might well behave in unacceptable ways. Self-haters are always in trouble.

Before you stick your head in the oven, let me try to persuade you that the world has not come to an end. Homosexuals, who hopefully understand more about themselves and have gained in self-respect, may or may not have full, creative, loving, responsible lives to the same degree as anyone else; what happens will depend in large part on how parents and grandparents react. If you express disgust, anger, or rejection, along with a good part of the rest of society, chances are not very great that this person, who wants love and understanding as much as anyone else, will become a happy, construc-tive member of society. If, on the other hand, you learn to accept the fact that homosexuality is not a disease, and if you recall that in every period of human history homosexuality has existed and that the world has been enriched by the genius of homosexuals in the arts, sci-ences, government, teaching, philosophy, and all other human endeavors, you may be able to feel reassured. It is also true that there are as many stable marriages among gay couples as among heterosexuals. So if you can give up the teachings of your childhood and youth, hopefully you will be able to tell your grandchild your love is unconditional.

This is not to suggest that we need feel guilty about

the terror of AIDS, being disappointed about not having any great-grandchildren if this is an only grandchild (gay couples are adopting more often), and feeling strange and uneasy at first. That's normal for our generation.

After the shock and misgivings and fears, grandparents can then do what they do best by saying, "You are my beloved grandchild and I want to be part of your life for as long as I live."

One letter which I cherish was from a grandma who wrote, "I thought I'd have to put my head in the oven when my grandson brought his partner to meet me. I'm glad I didn't—his friend is a lovely person and takes care of my taxes free of charge!"

Is It Our Money
or Theirs?

I WAS TALKING TO A YOUNG FRIEND ON THE PHONE. She was telling me how difficult it was to work part-time so she could be with her one-year-old son. She doesn't really want day care, and the baby-sitters cost half her salary. She and her husband find themselves unable to pay all their bills and are very worried about the future. Then Mary said: "I called my mother and asked her to send me a thousand dollars. I shouldn't have had to ask; she and my father have plenty of money. I can't understand why they don't just give it to us without being asked."

I didn't say anything—except I was sorry for their financial stress. But later on, because I am the age of her parents, I did a double take; why should she *expect* them to give her money? Whatever they have, they earned. They are now retired and want to enjoy the fruits of their labor. They don't *owe* Mary anything.

My husband and I give money to our divorced daughter and our granddaughter—there are thousands of parents and grandparents who find their children and grandchildren in far worse financial straits than when they were young, and who, however reluctantly and fearfully (because of concern for our own futures) don't have to be asked to help when the need is legitimate. My daughter wishes she could be independent. If she ever said, "You *owe* me," that would probably be a greater strain on our relationship than when she was a barefoot hippy in the streets of New York in the 1960s!

Whenever a young person uses the words "they owe me," I feel sure that what we are dealing with is old business. Mary feels her parents were neglectful and rejecting when she was a child. She always had the hope that if she were "good" she would get their attention and affection. She grew up to be a terrific person, happily married, miraculously a good mother despite her own experiences as a child, and a great success in her profession. Unconsciously she feels that since she measured up in every way possible her parents should now love her. They haven't changed; they are still ungiving. Mary's fury is not from today or yesterday but from long ago.

None of us ever want to hear our progeny tell us we "owe" them. At first glance it is infuriating. But the truth is that if our daughter felt she should expect our help, I would want to know why. She might need our help, but if she felt we owed her, I would wonder when and where we had failed long before. Had we expected too much? Had we ever indicated that love was tied to performance? Behind the "you owe me" is the statement "you never really were satisfied with me and nothing I've done has changed that."

It's not easy for any of us to give a lot of financial help when we have our own terror of financial dependency—but where there is mutual love and respect we do what we can. But if the word "owe" comes into the conversation I'd say it is time to try some honest talk about why; it may be our first chance to learn more about this demanding person who must have been an unhappy child.

But there is another indication of a neurotic history and that is when extremely wealthy parents or grandparents refuse to ever offer assistance; "not a penny until I die!" is the attitude. Also undoubtedly some other even earlier emotional trauma. Also sad. When money becomes a substitute for love *everyone* is in deep trouble.

When Sisters Live Together

THERE ARE A LOT OF OLDER PEOPLE LIVING IN MY
neighborhood, and I often see older women, usually two
together. I always know (or think I do) when they are
widowed sisters living together because more often than
not they seem to be arguing—using a tone of voice that
married couples undoubtedly use during disagreements
but less publicly. I think the difference is that spouses
didn't meet each other until adulthood, whereas sisters
have a history that probably includes early rivalries, jeal-
ousies, all the normal conflicts of siblings, struggling for
special and unconditional love from parents.

I always assume they are sisters because friends are
rarely so open with disgust, anger, criticism. I don't
know why I have never noticed this frequent rancor
between older brothers—I think fewer of them probably live as long and alone and don't tend to join forces
as often. Maybe sisters are just more open about their
feelings.

Do I think they hate each other? Not at all. I know
that I don't notice when they are being charming to each
other. What interests me is that the solution of living

together may have many advantages, both financially and emotionally, but it can't often be easy.

When sisters move in together, it is likely they may both be feeling lonely. They are not strangers to each other and have thousands of common memories. It seems like an ideal solution to their problems of aging— companionship, being able to care for each other, pooling resources. But when any two people live together, some conflict is inevitable.

But the reason I notice the degree of the anger I see is that I imagine neither sister has fully taken into account the importance of their shared past. Who is older and who is younger? How did the older one feel when the younger was born? Did their parents make comparisons so that they were rivals? Did one take advantage of the other? Was one more manipulative? Do they each feel the parents loved the other one better? It's a good idea to talk about this history with a great deal of candor, to clear the air of old wounds. Every relationship calls for compromise, mutual respect and communication.

The other day I was visiting a friend in the hospital. There was a crippled elderly woman in the corridor desperately asking the nurses for information about her husband, then being operated on. She wept and said to me, "Such a good man, such a good man." I thought how terrible it was that, sick and old herself, she seemed so utterly alone in this crisis. Then a woman about her age came briskly along the hall. They hugged each other; the wife cried harder. The second woman went up to the nurses' station and in a strong and authoritative voice said, "I'm her sister, and you have got to get her some information. She is not well herself, and it is cruel not to pay attention to her." Within a minute or two, they were both being told, "He's out of surgery, in the recovery room, and everything is all right."

That's the other and most important part of sisterhood. Whatever "old business" there may be, there is also a profound caring, a marvelous capacity to fight for and protect each other. Nothing new; ambivalence is always part of sibling relationships.

I Remain Shamelessly Romantic

AMONG ANY NUMBER OF REASONS WHY I AM GLAD I was born in the 1920s is the fact that I remain an unreconstructed romantic. On the visit of Princess Di to the poor and the wounded in New York, I was reminded of how I got up at five in the morning to watch her wedding, and the terrible pain in my child's soul when there was any suggestion that she and the Prince of Wales did not live happily ever after. I want desperately to go on believing in true love, even as I live in the midst of an avalanche of divorces. Where, oh where, are the dreams of my childhood, when no one ever told me there were not very many people walking into the sunset of life still passionately in love?

But I have just had a lesson in the fact that memory is faulty and that I really have changed since I was young. There is a cable television station that shows old movies of my adolescent years almost all day long, and what a shock it has been. There I find Cary Grant and Irene Dunne as silly and fake as can be, never telling each other the truth; there I find Jeanette MacDonald and Nelson Eddy, and Ginger Rogers and Fred Astaire,

going through complications and misunderstandings that
outdo Romeo and Juliet; and then there is Ruby Keeler
telling Dick Powell she can't marry him because he can't
dance, followed by a totally irrelevant Busby Berkeley
dance number peformed by thousands.

My movies were arch, childish, silly, and implausible.
Instead of hours of happy nostalgia, I shamefully found
myself wishing they would all be honest and open, tell
each other the truth, go to bed, fight, make up, and
make it clear they would always have problems—just
what I now know about life!

It occurs to me that I will never stop being a romantic,
absolutely convinced that happy endings—and beginnings—can be not only happy but quite beautiful. However, I no longer hope that princes and princesses will
stay in love, in perfect harmony forever. Now I find
romance in more supposedly ordinary things which are
not ordinary at all.

A daughter sends me a book of poetry, privately published after her mother's death; it is called *Written in
View of the 59th St. Bridge*, by Alice Donna Crouse, in
which she has written odes of love and appreciation to
her nurses and doctors, while she is dying at Memorial
Hospital in New York. Now I understand *that* is romantic and what romance really means is the eternal
quest for courage, dignity, love, in an imperfect world.

Dorothea is ninety. She has two knee replacements
and any number of other consequences of the aging
process. A few weeks ago she married Sam, ninety-two.
They were high-school sweethearts, but went in different directions and married other people. Now both wid-

owed, they have again fallen in love. In their new apartment there will be a wheelchair and a walker, but Dorothea asked her seventy-year-old daughter to buy her some new lingerie. They are taking a nurse's aide along on the honeymoon, but the way they looked at each other at the wedding, they could have been high-school kids again. A cousin asked them why they were bothering to get married—why didn't they just enjoy each other's company? Dorothea's answer was, with a mischievous twinkle, "Good heavens, honey, suppose I get pregnant!" *That's* romantic.

Dealing With Anger

TRY TO GET THIS PICTURE: SOMEHOW I HAVE MAN-
aged to lower my stiff and overweight body to the hall
floor in my apartment. I had bought a piece of carpeting
to be used as a hall runner to cover holes in the overall
carpeting that would cost thousands of dollars to replace,
which I don't have readily available. My husband had
promised me this morning that he'd come home early
to help me with binding the carpet and then hammering
in the carpet tacks because I have arthritis in both knees,
and getting up and down is now painful, if not entirely
impossible. But what I have discovered, now that I am
on the floor, is that I can't get up. I started this project
two hours after the expected arrival of my helpmate,
and now I am fuming, I'm in a rage. I mutter about his
selfishness and his thoughtlessness, and I feel terribly
sorry for myself. I realize that I am going to have to sit
on the floor until he comes home to help me get up.
I've done only half the job, and my back is killing me.
When That Man walks in the door, boy, is he going to
get it.

The door opens. I see at once that he is carrying a

bunch of my favorite flowers. He is contrite; he says he was sure I wouldn't start without him. Now I am twice as angry because I can't yell at him.

Happily married couples recognize this as a normal afternoon. Widowed men and women, I'm sure, are thinking, "That ungrateful wretch—she still has her spouse; she should appreciate her good fortune."

Absolutely true. I laugh. I acknowledge how mad I was getting. Together we manage to get me to a standing position—and I thank him for the flowers. I know how lucky I am—and I almost never forget the anguish of some of my lonely friends.

But for those of us who are still married to our best friend, and who have weathered some of the awful crises and hazards of a long life together, and wouldn't go through some of it again for love or money, but think a good deal about what it will be like when one of us dies and the other is left alone, I think it's important not to avoid confrontations just because this fear becomes more and more real as we get older and witness so many new widowhoods.

It is impossible to live in a close relationship without frustration, without losing patience, without someone being thoughtless—without conflict. The problem is that we are human. It is pointless to try to avoid confrontations—if we deny our anger or hurt feelings, if we try to hold our tempers, we will destroy the very thing we want so much to hold on to: a living, breathing, genuine relationship of intense communication and love.

I took my flowers and was grateful he was home safely,

and we went on from that crisis, knowing there would be others, but never forgetting to affirm the love. We take the bad moments, we cherish the good ones, and whatever happens in the future there will be no regrets about anger and misunderstanding. It is part of the package. It is part of being fully alive.

Divorce After Sixty

AT FIRST I THOUGHT HE WAS JUST AN OLD MAN, sitting on a park bench, feeding some pigeons—but there was something familiar about the face. He smiled and said, "I'm not surprised you don't recognize me— we haven't seen each other for about twenty years." I knew immediately it was Martin, best man at our wedding forty-five years ago. We had lost touch, living far apart, losing common interests. "Molly and I are getting a divorce." What a shock! This "old man" was maybe two years older than I; he and Molly had been married two years before my husband and myself. Molly had been my confidante, my cheerleader during Larry's and my courtship. They had three sons, now in their late thirties or early forties. The Perfect Marriage.

Although I find it very hard to condone divorces of convenience when there are young children (by that I mean where there has not been a major, pathological problem), I can understand that (mostly) young men may find they have gotten more than they bargained for and find marriage too binding. It's all so easy now. I can even understand those (mostly men, but some women) who, in their forties and early fifties, feel mortality breathing down their necks and think a new career or a younger lover will help them to deny the reality of getting older. But when it comes to people married almost fifty years and longer, I find myself totally at a loss to understand, if the marriage has seemed as good as or better than most.

Nobody but the principals can know the secret complexities, but having lived through plenty of pain myself, I find it hard to believe that the work of staying married so long doesn't pay off for some couples.

A friend of mine, a psychiatrist, says at regular intervals to remind those of us in the psychological professions how limited is our understanding of the mysteries of the human soul, "The longer I treat patients and study psychology, the less I know about human beings."

In spite of not understanding the causes too well, I have some clues. Divorce after sixty seems to happen most often when communication about feelings has been blocked; divorce after sixty is likely if one or both partners cannot accept the changes that come with age. A little arthritis here, a little heart trouble there, a hysterectomy that seems to have lowered the capacity for orgasm, lots of gray hair and lines, while Dr. Ruth talks gaily about sex at ninety, and in a desperate attempt to deny the aging process, one still may search for greener fields to lift a less passionate libido. What this implies is an unwillingness to change, to accept the part of reality that may be inevitable, and to work at discovering new sources of tenderness and caring. Divorce after sixty is likely to mean one or both partners feel imprisoned—

not enough space between them to breathe, too much togetherness, too much interdependence, and no separate hobbies, trips, or learning experiences. Boredom from passivity; too *much* acceptance of limitations.

For those of us bearing down on seventy, still reasonably happily married or, praise be, madly in love, let these thoughts be a lesson. It's never too late to nourish a marriage that's worth saving.

When Our Children Divorce

A MOST DISTURBING EVENT IS TAKING PLACE: there is more and more evidence as the children of divorce multiply and grow up that they are almost always left with a residue of emotional disturbance. My suspicions were first aroused when author Jill Krementz was writing a book in which she interviewed children of divorce.* We had each written children's books about the death of a parent and one day Jill called and said, "Eda, this has come as a great shock, but these children are suffering more than if a parent had died!" I began to get a personal glimpse of the havoc of divorce on children when my own grandchild became a victim. In January 1989, the *New York Times Magazine* featured an important article by Judith Wallerstein, working on a long-term project in California, which suggested very strongly that even after ten or fifteen years the wounds could still be considerable.

Does that shock any of us over sixty? I doubt it; we have been having misgivings for a long time.

I used to think that my concern about divorce where

How It Feels When Parents Divorce (Knopf, 1984).

children were involved was my just being old-fashioned; after all, in all the years of my growing up I can't recall a single divorce, and among my married friends, in my age group, a divorce was still most unusual.

I think I was also slow to be too concerned because in the 1940s and 1950s most child experts were saying that, after all, it was better for children to live through a divorce than to live with people who didn't love each other or even hated each other. I think most of us would still agree that divorce is a necessary tool where one of the parents is psychotic, alcoholic, abusive, or plagued by any other truly serious problem. But many of us are now concluding that when close to fifty percent of the children in any classroom come from single-parent families, something else has happened. Divorce has become an easy way out—a socially acceptable way to be irresponsible. My guess is that perhaps half of the divorces where children are concerned might have been avoided without trauma to the children, if both parents had worked hard to learn to live together, as well as creatively discovering ways to have "separate space" in their lives without divorcing. When I recently put forth such a notion in *Woman's Day* I received more than three hundred letters, all agreeing (divorced parents, teachers, school principals, and pediatricians among them) except for one dissenter.

We have been frightened, unhappy—often terribly angry—when our children and grandchildren have lived through one or more divorces. There is nothing we can do about the fact, but we can help with the consequences. We can intervene by trying to help the children understand their own feelings, their parents' problems, the fact that children are far from alone, and that when their unhappiness is honestly faced they can become stronger and better able to survive. Talk, read books for children on divorce together, and make it clear you are always available to listen to their problems. Often the intervention of grandparents can help to make a child feel safe again.

Facing Up to a Friend's Illness

THE HUSBAND OF A FRIEND WHO HAS ALZHEIMER'S disease wrote me: "Mary can't even feed herself. She doesn't know me. I can't understand anything she says. How could this happen to the wonderful person she was? This is sadder than death."

Indeed it is. The only positive fact in this situation is that John and Mary have been living well and happily in a residence for older people, and he can continue to live in an apartment while Mary is getting constant care in the nursing home affiliate. But the tragedy is monumental. Mary was my boss many, many years ago. We worked together in a department of mental-health education. I still remember going to her home to be interviewed, and I met this gracious, charming woman. We sat in her flower garden drinking iced tea. Gardening was her passion. In all the years we worked together there was never a single argument—she was a booster of everyone around her. I had visited her about a year ago, when she was enjoying retirement to the fullest. There were at least five different bird feeders outside her garden apartment and a miniature flower bed, a reminder of her special love.

I never knew a woman to be so close to, so adoring of, her two daughters-in-law. They were surely as much her children as her sons. Until Alzheimer's struck, suddenly, like lightning, she and John kept a family home in the Adirondack Mountains, where the whole family met for Christmas and summer holidays.

What Mary and I did together, mostly, was to meet with parents and talk about childraising. She was such a nurturer herself that she made it possible for other parents to give as much as she gave to their own children. She was so loved by so many.

How can we deal with this awful challenge? Children, spouses, the patient him- or herself? Practically, there are more resources for help than ever before—not enough, but an important beginning: day care for patients who can still function reasonably well; specialized institutional care; more and more research to help us understand and hopefully in the future to provide some medical help; counseling and guidance for families; and a growing number of support groups for relatives. When we are faced with this dreadful reality, we need to call on all the help we can possibly get.

But beyond the day-by-day issues, something else has to happen as well. I already mourn for my friend Mary, for hers is a death in life. There is nothing I can do for her. But I try to think of things she would want me to do, if she could tell me—and of course, first on the list is to keep in touch with John. And then to offer my friendship to her children and grandchildren, where my greatest asset is that I can tell stories about all the wonderful ways in which Mary has helped others. I can remember with them some of her triumphs they may not know about, having to do with her career. She and I once worked on a New York State Regents Committee on Education, and I can tell stories about the wise and funny and loving things she said, how much she was respected and loved by all of us.

I need to think about her garden—not only the one behind her home but the way in which her life was a garden. I need to remember that she had just about the best of everything until she was eighty-one, which is more than we can say for most people. And the message of this saddest news is that each of us must make the most and the best of the years that we have, so while there may be grief, there will not be any regrets.

An Open Letter
to the Tooth Fairy

In spite of Martha Raye I am devastated. I've got the Tooth Trauma. It happened all of a sudden; bridges are falling apart all over the country and have become part of the social scene. My scene resulted in an "upper" that hurts, doesn't fit, and doesn't bite. Oatmeal and applesauce days. I never knew I cared so much—but I do.

If I'd been in a car accident at thirty and had to have false teeth thereafter, it would not have been so traumatic. But at sixty-seven it is just one more sign of inexorable deterioration.

Where is my Tooth Fairy? When I was a child ten cents was the going rate for selling her a tooth undercover. Later it went to twenty-five when it was for my second set of teeth. Now I understand Tooth Fairies may be going out of business because kids expect to find a Mercedes Benz under the pillow. The thing is, I gave those teeth up without a qualm—even joyously— because they meant I was growing up. The ones that are gone now mean I have been growing for much too long. I beg my Tooth Fairy to return the ones I gave up so willingly. I will find a place for them, somehow— size no longer matters at all.

My neighbor across the hall tells me when she got her upper plate five years ago, at seventy, it took her a whole year to get over the accompanying depression. The whole thing seems absurd and selfish and self-pitying. People are being mugged and killed; people are starving; people are freezing in the streets. How can I fuss about not being able to chew and looking like a character in *Halloween III* when I open my mouth?

I am sure some people with dentures (the younger the better because it was less indicative of their aging) have probably concluded I am out of my mind. They haven't minded a bit; they are comfortable; they can even eat corn and steak. But I can't help it. I feel like Samson losing his hair—my strength is gone!

When I was a nursery-school teacher about one hundred years ago, I remember that we used to give carrot and celery sticks to the aggressive children. We would have long, dramatic discussions of biting hard and making a lot of noise. Some kids still bit other children but I recall that we cut that down about eighty percent through our vegetable therapy. When we were too young to fight with words or hands or feet, we could protect ourselves and express our displeasure at the behavior of others by biting them. Presumably that stage passed once we discovered better means of self-defense and expressing anger. But maybe, deep-down, some of us still have a primitive feeling that our teeth are powerful weapons for survival. Whatever neurotic force is driving me, I am having a hard time. I keep telling myself my fingers can still walk across the typewriter keys. But I still wish the Tooth Fairy would hear my plea and I'd find my first teeth under the pillow.

What Can Be Done
About Aged-Parent Abuse

IT BECAME NECESSARY A FEW MONTHS AGO FOR ME
to take over my ninety-three-year-old father's finances.
I applied to have his Social Security checks sent to me,
since I would now be paying all his bills. I was very
pleased and surprised to discover that this wasn't such
an easy transfer—someone down there in the bureaucracy is really watching out for my father's interests! I
had to fill out a complicated application, he was notified
that he could object, and I was informed that his checks
would have to be put in a separate account and that at
the end of each year I would be held accountable for
all expenditures.

I think that's just wonderful; there are too many re-
ports these days, as people are living well into their
nineties and even longer, of horrendous abuse of parents' rights, freedom, dignity, and financial assets.

I receive many letters from people caught in this awful
trap. In one case an elderly woman was accused by her
son of having called his probation officer to tell him he
was again taking drugs. The mother had not done this,

but is so frightened that her son will try to kill her that she hides alone in a single room, communicating with no one. That's extreme—much more common is this kind of story: When her husband died and she was feeling totally devastated, a woman of seventy-two was invited to come and live with her daughter and son-in-law. Shortly thereafter she became seriously ill, at which point she was left in a room with no telephone and fed leftover scraps, and all her mail was intercepted. Now that Social Security has made it very clear to me that I had better toe the line, I don't know how the son-in-law was able to steal every check she was receiving, but he did. After a year in which she almost died, a suspicious sister descended on the house with a court order for a search, and the abused invalid is now living with this sister.

It is not only children who abuse old people. In another letter a woman tells me of a second husband who turned out to be a gambler, beat her, and left her penniless and alone at seventy-six. A man wrote to say that he had a stroke and became totally dependent on others for his care; his sister screamed at him constantly, sometimes withheld his medications, would not call the doctor when he pleaded for help, fed him so quickly that he choked and slobbered, and would take the food away when he was still hungry. She finally, after all his financial resources were gone, put him in a nursing home, and it was there that one of the aides helped him to write to me.

There are thousands of such stories—the question is what can be done about it. I am not without sympathy for the caregivers; the burdens can be so excessive as to create terrible anger. The answer to that is that there must be a system of communal concern, group support, for families who become responsible for the aged and infirm.

But far more important, each of us must think carefully about our futures and make necessary provisions and safeguards in relation to money as well as ongoing care. One woman, living with children who have become quite cruel, wrote, "How much more convenient it would be if I would just die, melt away—but how?" A man wrote, "I am not afraid of dying, only of the indignities, the anger I create in others by my helplessness."

Whatever our resources, each of us must be thinking and planning long before we become dependent on others to decide where we want to live and what we want to do. Many with the financial means are choosing residences that will provide perpetual care; those with fewer resources need to seek the help of social agencies to make plans for the future.

We need to be aware, no matter how sure we are that we have a loving family, that changes do occur, and we should see to it that at least several friends and relatives are always in touch with us, wherever we may be.

The majority of caregivers are generous and compassionate, but we must prepare ourselves for those few who might make our twilight years unbearable. Once, while I was visiting a nursing home to see an aunt, there was a woman crying and fighting with her children, who were trying to place her in this institution. My aunt commented, "She doesn't know what's good for her. Here, at least, there are always outsiders who come in, so you can tell someone if you are mistreated. I feel safer here than I would in some private house like a prisoner."

This is a sad commentary, but a subject we must think about and plan for, long before we may become dependent on others.

The Death of an Adult Child

SOME YEARS AGO MY HUSBAND AND I WERE charmed by a singer at a summer resort. When we complimented her and said how much we had enjoyed her performance, she replied bitterly, "It's all an act. Frankly I'd like to die."

She was a widow who had devoted herself to her daughter, a brilliant and beautiful child. Two months before our meeting, this daughter, always in excellent health, eagerly looking forward to her high-school prom, had gotten some mysterious illness and died within three days. "I sing and smile," she told us, "and then I go back to my room and wish I had the courage to kill myself. There is nothing left to live for—my life is over."

Did we murmur small sounds of sympathy? Not on your life! Well, that's not quite true—we did of course acknowledge the anguish she was going through—but then my husband (a psychologist who has worked extensively with people in crisis) said, "Well, I'm sure your daughter would be overjoyed to hear how you are honoring her memory!"

Sonia looked startled, then furious, and walked away without a word. A few hours later she found Larry and said, "What did you mean by what you said?" That question was the first step toward recovery; the pain would be with her for the rest of her life, but she would now begin to celebrate her daughter's life rather than her death.

Larry asked Sonia to talk about her daughter: what were her favorite subjects in school; what kinds of friends did she have; what did they do together to have fun; did her daughter have special dreams for the future? "The only way you can keep some part of her inside you forever is to think about what she would have liked you to do, in her memory," my husband told Sonia. They spent several hours the next day talking about the things Sonia might do. Her daughter had urged Sonia to audition for a Broadway musical; her daughter was planning to go to a college where she would major in architectural design; her daughter had been working as a volunteer an afternoon a week on the pediatric service of a hospital. Sonia, now thoughtful and quiet, said, "When this gig is over, I'm going home and I'm going to get a new agent who believes in my talent as much as Jessie did. Then I'm going to take over her volunteer assignment. And I'm going to create a small grant to the college she hoped to go to, in the architecture department."

We didn't see or hear from Sonia for about a year and a half, until, with great surprise, we discovered she

was in a musical at a summer music tent. We went back-
stage and she met us with shining eyes. She said, "I even
have a boyfriend now!"

Losing an adult child at whatever age it happens is a
terrible tragedy. It goes against nature. It seems incon-
ceivable that a child could die before a parent. And while
a period of terrible grief and mourning is appropriate
for such a loss, what we need to remember is that the
only way to honor and keep close to the memory of this
child is to celebrate what was most precious about that
life, to give that child continued "life" through fulfilling
his or her dreams.

One grandmother said she couldn't bear to visit her
son's children after his death. She thereby robbed herself of his immortality, and her grandchildren felt a
second loss and rejection. If an adult child dies leaving grandchildren behind, our opportunities for turning
grief into meaning and purpose are even greater. Who
better than a parent to keep memory alive, to give a
child's children a lasting legacy?

After much persuasion and the promise that her second son would go with her, this frightened grandmother
went to visit her four grandchildren, who rushed toward
her, almost knocking her over, hugging and kissing her.
She later said, "They looked so much like David!
Especially the two girls. And when they called me
'Grandma,' and showed me how much they needed me
to tell them about their father when he was a child, I
wondered what I had been so afraid of."

When a child dies it is natural to be afraid of any
further pain. For a while we may just want to crawl into

a hole and lick our wounds. But then we need to have the courage to say to ourselves: "I'm still here. I can carry on the unfinished life. I can fulfill some of the dreams and give the love my child would have given. I can make that life *count*." And in that sense of purpose and the good we do, we remain forever in touch with the child we thought we had lost.

Keeping Connected to Young People

I SOMETIMES DO THINGS I SWORE I WOULD NEVER do. It's hard even to admit it, when I recall how I hated older people who did such things when I was young— but here it is: I sometimes lump all young people together and curse them out. When a door is slammed in my face, or when someone young doesn't say "thank you" or "excuse me," or when someone under forty doesn't get up for a lame old man on a bus, I am ashamed to say I often mutter under my breath, "God save me from the younger generation."

I remember how angry I would be when older people showed this kind of prejudice when I was a member of the younger generation—people said we were all selfish, rude, thoughtless, spoiled, and lazy, and lectured us about their work ethic (six days a week, dawn to dusk in a poorly heated, un-air-conditioned sweat shop, etc., etc.). We didn't know the meaning of hard work; we didn't appreciate frozen food, dishwashers, and laundromats; we were thoughtless, rude, and lazy. We got pretty mad, as I recall.

I don't want to be that kind of critical, intolerant old

person. I know that keeping as young and alive as I can
for as long as I can requires a feeling of loving con-
nectedness to younger people. I constantly chastise myself for blaming "the younger generation" for behavior
that annoys and upsets me. I want to look tenderly upon
the human race, regardless of race, creed, religion, or
age.

What I need to remember is that despite all the social
changes that have taken place, despite the higher divorce
rate, the great increase in the number of working mothers, and the general frenzy of life today, nice people are
nice people, at any age and we are far closer to the needs
and feelings and struggles of younger people than we
sometimes remember.

For every thoughtless person who slams a door or
doesn't give us a seat there are thousands of others who
remember and are grateful for our efforts and dreams
and who have the same dreams for a good and decent
life.

What matters about the younger generation is that
life is harder and more frightening for them than it ever
was for us and they need us to praise their courage and
their struggles. We ought to be out there on the bar-
ricades fighting for more good day-care centers and less
radon under their backyards, fewer missiles scaring their
children and more vegetables that aren't poisoned with
chemicals, so they have more time to hold their children
on their laps and build sand castles and read *Winnie the
Pooh*. Next time someone young almost knocks me over
on the street, I am going to remind myself that most of
"the younger generation" is simply me, thirty or forty
years ago, but facing bigger problems.

Progress Sometimes
Drives Me Crazy

I HAVE A WONDERFUL LITTLE RADIO; YOU TURN A knob and in one hour the radio turns itself off. There is no clock, no dials saying "slumber" and "sleep" and "snooze." It's about thirty years old. It also has a place for an earplug so I can listen without waking up my husband. I need a new radio for my office. I've been to every radio store within a ten-mile radius of home. I have not yet found a single radio that I can understand or manage. There are at least ten dials and no earplug. Or an earplug but no sleep turn-off. Each one looks like the panel on a 747.

As does every automobile. We don't own a car (anyone in Manhattan who does is insane or a millionaire) and when we try to rent a car, I want you to know it is now *impossible* to rent one with windows you can roll down manually. And if I study the dials to figure out where the windshield wipers are, I will surely run into the first truck or car I encounter. When my husband left me in a car one time and absent-mindedly took the keys, I nearly suffocated and became hysterically claustrophobic while I waited. Why aren't we allowed to turn the windows down or up non-electronically? I'm sure I don't know.

The reason I don't have a microwave or a dishwasher is that I could never learn to use them. The old washing machines were wonderful; "hot" and "cold," "off" and "on," "regular" and "delicate," and that was it. Without an engineering degree I don't know how anyone manages anymore. I have never used my telephone credit card. I cannot understand the bank's fast money-machine system. I have never used my three-year-old VCR.

There is this insane idea that complicated is better. I wanted to buy some wall hooks recently. They used to lie in a box and you picked out however many you wanted. Now two hooks come in a plastic package. It took me half an hour with scissors and a knife, cursing all the way, to open the package. At a time when plastic will soon take over the world, everything we buy is in a plastic container because some damn person in advertising got the idea that it wasn't important what was inside a wrapping as long as the outside was gorgeous.

The problem is, we are all sheep. We, who are old, know that once upon a time, before Madison Avenue and the apparent hunger for complexity on the part of younger generations, it was easy to drive a car or open a package of sliced ham or read a watch for the time of day, not the month and year, and have plenty of time for simple pleasures. I would like to form an association to complain to Detroit about the car windows. That would at least be a start. Are you with me?

Different Ways
of Dealing
With a Serious Illness

JENNY WAS ABOUT AS SICK AS ANYONE COULD BE. She had a deadly form of cancer and little hope of surviving for more than a few months. Every time the doctors told her they had used as much radiation and chemotherapy as they could, Jenny would go running to other doctors. She insisted on several exploratory operations, which doctors told her would be more hazardous than useful. She went on one crazy diet after another—all extreme, all advocated by amateurs. She tried hypnosis, acupuncture, and meditation, all useful in some situations, but she was too sick for these kinds of interventions. She traveled far and wide to every possible court of last resort, but to no avail.

At one point, when she was in a great deal of pain in the hospital, she asked for the chaplain. The young man who appeared at her bedside was both a minister and a psychologist. He was easy to talk to, and Jenny was partly drugged and said more than she had to anyone else. She told him she had had a terrible childhood, with abusive parents; she told him she had reached a feeling of great happiness only when she went to work as an assistant director of an art museum, after majoring in art history in college. And then she fell in love with a man ten years older, who asked her to follow him to another city, giving up her work. He wanted children. Jenny had three miscarriages and desperately longed to go back to her job. Then she got cancer.

If medical science has learned anything in the past few decades, it is that under severe emotional stress the immune system can break down, changing the body's chemistry, making one more vulnerable to almost any serious disease. Surely other factors cause illness (smoking, genetics, asbestos in the ceiling, additives in food, and car emissions, to name a few) but also traumatic life experiences, especially among people who are already vulnerable by the nature of their past experiences.

There is no reason to assume that examining her inner life would have saved Jenny. There is also no reason to believe it might not have extended her life, made it more rich and rewarding, maybe even brought about a remission. I happen to have witnessed a great many such miracles myself.*

The point is that whenever we are seriously, frighteningly ill, we need to use every possible resource for trying to get well. Medical treatment first, of course, and any other resources represented by responsible, eth-

---

*Through the research of my husband, Lawrence LeShan, as described in his *Cancer as a Turning Point* (New American Library, 1989).

ical people. But *not* to be ignored are the factors that keep us from bringing our own best healing processes into play. We need to put up a fight to find out where we have cheated ourselves out of fulfillment, when we have given so much more to others than to ourselves.

My husband, who visits very sick people frequently in hospitals, is always delighted when the nurses and relatives hate him on sight! He knows that the person he has come to see is not sweet and gentle and quiet and passive and accepting, but has become a warrior in his or her own defense. Nothing gets the immune system fighting harder than taking control of one's life and getting to know oneself better.

Some Mental Exercises
When Depression Hits

ONE OF THE MANY ADVANTAGES OF BEING MAR-
ried to my husband is that he teaches people to meditate
and to play "games" which can help them face illness,
depression, and other life crises. If you are feeling low,
or sense a need to get more in touch with your feelings,
get yourself some paper and a pencil. Here are some
exercises for the mind and the heart:

> Write a letter to yourself about a time when you
> were a child and were told you were naughty be-
> cause you misbehaved. What would you tell that
> child, now?
>
> Close your eyes and imagine a place that you would
> consider "a safe harbor," a place where you could
> feel safe and happy, either imaginary or real. What
> would it be like, or what was it like?
>
> Imagine that a fairy godmother comes to you. You
> can have any three wishes you want. What would
> they be?
>
> What was the worst thing that ever happened to
> you?

What was the happiest time?

Sit back comfortably and close your eyes. Pretend there is a giant movie screen in front of you, and let images float through your mind of things you would love to do, places you would like to go, things you would like to learn.

Pretend it's your birthday and you are your own very best friend; what would you give yourself?

Write down what you would like people to say about you at your own funeral. What would you like on your gravestone; what would come closest to your ideal self?

Write a letter to your mother, your father; you are a child and you want them to understand you better.

Write, "From my childhood I love to remember . . ."; "From my childhood I hate to remember . . ."

Pretend you are a college freshman; what subjects would you want to study? Would you plan a different life than the one you have had or would you do the same things over again?

Write a letter to your spouse, to your grown children, anyone who was or is important to you. How do you want them to remember you? Are there things for which you need their forgiveness? Your own forgiveness? What are you most proud of? What are your regrets?

You need to try to be as spontaneous as possible; don't think—write! There is no value in such games unless you allow yourself to learn about yourself. Hopefully some of what you learn may shock you into action. Inner thoughts are not enough to get us through the rough spots in life—action, doing, is the answer.

After one of my husband's seminars, in which I did these exercises, I wrote a play. I felt so much better afterwards!

If You Dare to Die
Before Me,
I'll Kill You

A FRIEND OF MIND TOLD ME THAT HE AND HIS WIFE were having a very hard time with his widowed mother-in-law, who was still in deep mourning a year after her husband's death and was forcing her daughter into the role of total, full-time caretaker. She is seventy years old, in excellent health, and yet is refusing to take any responsibility for her own life, apparently unable to move back into any semblance of a normal life.

"Of course we understood how grief-stricken she was—after all, my wife had also lost a beloved father, but now we are quite appalled by the fact that rather than any signs of recovery, my mother-in-law is regressing," he told me.

All I did was ask one simple question: "Since your father-in-law's death, has his wife ever screamed her bloody head off, cursing him out for leaving her?" My friend was shocked. "Of course not," he said. "I don't think she has ever lost her temper in all the years I have known her, both married and widowed."

I often tell my husband that if he *dares* to die before me, I'll kill him! I cannot even imagine the depth of the grief I would experience, but one thing I know for sure: I would be screaming mad at him and would curse him out for having dared to desert me. That doesn't mean I am a horrible person—it means I'm normal. Whether expressed or repressed, it is a natural human instinct to cry out in anger and anguish when someone we love dies. It doesn't make any difference how the death occurred; a spouse might have been hit by a truck crossing a street legally, or struck by lightning. There is nothing rational about one's anger—it is just *there* and it is only when the widowed person cannot face or express or reveal this anger that the mourning period goes on and on, and the widowed person becomes more and more paralyzed and helpless.

This is true at every age level. It is very hard to help a child who has lost a parent face any anger at all; they feel lost and helpless and scared. But when one breaks through the terror of being angry, recovery begins. Suzy screamed, "I hate him! I hate him!" three months after her adored father died—and was then able to begin to face the future. It is just impossible not to have feelings of rejection, unreasonable as they may be. Liz asked me, "How could I be mad? He was such a wonderful father and I loved him so much," and then, suddenly, howled in fury, "He didn't love me, or he wouldn't have died!" From that point on it was possible to talk about normal anger arising out of great love and need.

I suggested to my friend that he and his wife try their darnedest to get his mother-in-law to go talk to someone at a crisis center or join a widows' support group. If they can't make any headway, they can gently but firmly begin to talk about all the normal feelings one has when a loved one dies—that it is normal to feel fury and rage, and this in no way makes the love and grief less real. Unfinished business always gets us in trouble, and so many times in life that unfinished business is anger we are afraid and ashamed to face.

Oh, how I would rant and rave and call my husband terrible names, and then I would probably cry most of the time for several months, allowing myself every natural emotion of grief, and then, reluctantly, I admit I'd go on with living.

When You're Alone
on a Holiday

THERE USED TO BE (ONE HUNDRED YEARS AGO, IT seems!) a restaurant in Manhattan, on Broadway, called the C. and L. It was a family kind of place and had excellent food, and I clearly remember a year when my husband and I decided to go there after the theater on New Year's Eve. We quickly noticed that there were a great many people sitting alone, looking very depressed and lonely. We were much younger—we hardly even noticed that they were mostly older people—but I remember feeling uneasy, unhappy. What I was reacting to, and came to understand only as I grew older, is that the older one gets the more likely one will be alone, especially on holidays.

Widowhood accounts for the largest number of those who suffer emotional distress at this time of year. And then there are the others whose closest friends and relatives have died or live too far away. Even friends or relatives who are still within reach are probably afraid to go out, or no longer drive, or have infirmities that make taking any kind of action difficult.

As I look back to that New Year's Eve and the unhappy faces, I must say that I at least understand the courage it must have taken for those single people to go out at all, to try to bring in the new year with some style.

A large percentage of the mail I get has to to do with loneliness, on holidays or any day. The problem is that as we get older we get some new tasks for which we are unprepared. Usually, when we are young, we are too busy raising children, working, entertaining, and visiting to have much time alone. We don't anticipate the new skills we will need, the greatest of which is to begin, hopefully, to appreciate the fact that every one of us has a companion from birth to death—ourselves, and that self can be a source of entertainment, pleasure, and comfort. It's a time to realize that we need to join groups, to find a support system. One man wrote me, "I have never asked anyone for help and I'm not going to start now." This attitude is misguided on two points; there is no shame in seeking companionship, and rather than focusing on what it can do for you, think of what you might contribute to the life of someone else.

Give yourself a special treat—call a distant friend or relative, even if they owe you a call or a letter. Work as a volunteer in a hospital at a time when staff is low because of the holidays. Take some lonely, shy teenager in your apartment building or neighborhood to a movie. Go to a Salvation Army center or a church where dinner is being served to homeless families and offer to help. Thinking of the needs of others is the best antidote to self-pity. Do something for somebody.

And most of all, be proud of yourself for having the courage to go on, no matter what the inner pain. That night at the restaurant, when midnight came, a woman at least in her eighties, impeccably dressed, raised a glass of champagne to herself and then toward us. There was such courage and dignity in her face that our eyes filled with tears. We were young, but we knew we had been witnesses to something very special.

Silence Can Be Golden

IT SEEMS TO ME WE HAVE GONE OVERBOARD ON THE subject of communication. For the past ten to twenty years I've gotten the feeling that experts in the psychological arts have been suggesting that the solution to every problem has been to talk to each other, express feelings honestly—COMMUNICATE. I submit with some shame that I have been as guilty of this as the next shrink type.

It has been occurring to me lately that while communicating about feelings can be very helpful, silence can be equally valuable, in the right places at the right times. I am hooked on people-watching, and when I was younger and quite a bit more stupid I always assumed that if I saw a couple eating in a restaurant and not talking to each other that meant they were unhappy. What has changed my mind is an increasing awareness of the silences that occur between me and my husband of forty-five years. It was a shock to realize, recently, that we had sat through an entire meal in almost total silence, and I know we are not unhappy! The truth is, our marriage was saved many times by successful communication but we no longer feel at all threatened by silences. When we have spent a great deal of time talking to other people and are incapable of the slightest social contact, it feels really good to be near each other without having to say a word.

Once I began to think about the value of silence I remembered that it wasn't always talking that healed our psychic wounds. Sitting far apart while reading or working in the same room, walking on a beach, watching birds at a feeder—even letting an argument go for a while so that each of us could get a better perspective on the issue—might very well solve the problem; there would have been time to think about the fact that whatever the problem, there were two sides to the matter.

Visiting someone in a hospital recently, I watched an elderly couple. The man was in a wheelchair, his wife sitting next to him in the visitors' room. For the half hour that I watched they never exchanged a word, just held hands and looked at each other, and once or twice the man patted his wife's face. The feeling of love was so thick in that room that I felt I was sharing in their communion and was shaken all day by their pain, their love, something sad and also joyful: the fullness of a human relationship.

There are times when we should not be afraid to be silent: when recovering from weariness, when needing some respite from being overpeopled, when needing time and space for our own inner thoughts. I think we have been inclined to feel guilty and think we are failing in a relationship if we leave each other alone—

separate in our thoughts and feelings—for a time. Maybe silence is especially important as we grow older. When we do communicate with words it ought to be when we have something to say—not just creating noise to avoid an inner quiet, which is communicating with ourselves.

The Season
to Celebrate Children

I LIKE THE HOLLY AND THE CHRISTMAS TREES AND
the Chanukah candles and Santa Claus. Only a Scrooge
could fail to be captured by the party atmosphere. But
what I like best, and wish there was more of, is that
what we celebrate is *children*, whatever our religion. But
what bothers me (and grandparents play an important
part in this) is that we tend to celebrate children by
stuffing them with holiday cookies and drowning them
in things—bicycles, talking dolls, and four-foot stuffed
animals. I happen to feel that *the* toy store of New York
City is something of an obscenity, with an overwhelming
number of items that cost over a thousand dollars. A
grandmother told me she took her granddaughter to
F.A.O. Schwarz and then to Macy's. She asked the child
which store she liked better and was startled to hear, "I
liked Macy's better because I think there are things there
you can afford to buy me."

I wish there were a little less hoopla, less focus on
presents, and a great deal more reflection on the fact
that at the present time children—children in general,

all children—are considered one of the lowest priorities by a great many people. We have fewer child-health clinics, a higher infant-mortality rate, more inadequate housing, and more overcrowded and ill-equipped schools than all the European democracies. There are surely better day-care facilities for single working parents in the Soviet Union. Shame on us! Tinsel and toys should not blind us to the fact that as older people our most important claim to immortality is to leave the world a better place for our greatest national resource, our kids, everybody's kids.

At the darkest time of the year, when the birth of a child is celebrated, when the laughter of children matters to so many, when just about every religion uses the darkest time of the year to create light and warmth for families, we need to ponder why, in the current climate of life, due to the tensions and worries of the time, there is a tendency to eliminate childhood, to make children grow up faster than ever before—to almost skip childhood altogether.

All the presents you can pile in the car when you visit your grandchildren won't matter a bit if you show your disappointment over a second-grader who is having trouble learning to read or a fifth-grader who doesn't get A's, or a high-schooler who is terrible at sports. The gift all children need from us—more from grandparents than anyone else—is the gift of unconditional love: "No matter what your weaknesses and strengths, no matter what your differences from others are, you are a special miracle." The current academic pressures on children all over this country are turning them into crippled teenagers, too easily drawn to drugs, to suicide, and to copping out. Our children know we don't care enough about their future to clean up the environment no matter what the cost. They know there are plenty of atomic bombs to wipe out the planet.

Give children security and love; show them you care about their futures, as well as buying them gifts. My granddaughter is getting a Greenpeace shirt this year to let her know I'm thinking about her future. She will also get a special dress with stars on it that she craves. Children cannot and should not be burdened with our grownup tasks of saving their futures.

Nothing
Is Simple Anymore

We who are getting older are not getting paranoid; it is really true that the world is now against us.

I put the garbage in the hall near the door to be taken to the incinerator. I stand it up in perfect balance; the garbage bag tips over. I hold on to a prescription with great care for three days and the first chance I get to go to the drugstore, the damn thing has disappeared. I imagine I had it in a pile of mail in the hall and put it in the mailbox by mistake. I hope the postman, who is young, won't bother to have it filled—it was for an old-age problem, which I don't wish to discuss any further.

A box of clips falls on the floor and opens. I wonder how I can bend down long enough to pick them up. I feel weary after writing a couple of columns and get myself a *large* glass of iced coffee, which I put on my desk. Needless to say I knock it over and there goes a whole day's work. I need to tell my aunt something important and her line is busy for six hours. I forget to write down the telephone number of a new doctor and can't find the magnifying glass so I can look it up in the phone book. I think I have misfiled two important papers and spend three hours trying to find them; they reappear later when I run into the kitchen, having smelled the tea kettle burning because I forgot all about it. The weatherman on TV warns it will rain all day, and I sweat in my boots and carry my umbrella through a day of blue sky and sunshine. The next day I pay no attention to the warnings of sleet and snow and spend the day trudging about with wet feet.

Finally, slowly, it begins to dawn on me: I am NOT the woman I once was, and I never will be again. Nothing is simple because I get tired more easily, am clumsier, and should feel lucky I still remember my name. What I also have come to understand is that whether or not things are simple anymore, I am *alive* and I'll settle for that.

A beloved friend, a poet, groans loudly over the telephone that total decay is upon her—she has had to stay in bed for three days; just could not get up, too exhausted to move. On further interrogation she admits that she has given four speeches in various parts of the United States within two weeks and has no household help at the age of seventy-seven. "Now everything is complicated," she tells me. Actually, going to bed for three days is exactly what she needed—a brilliant move on the part of her overtaxed body. When we cannot manage the same order in our lives we once enjoyed before vulnerability set in, we rage uselessly. Better to accept what is different and be glad for survival.

I went to the health-food store the other day and said to the clerk, "I need more of that vitamin that helps me remember better, but I can't remember its name." It would have been simpler if I'd remembered what I wanted, and the days are full of new complications, but at least I'm still here to deal with them.

II

MEMORIES

"Nothing can help us face the unknown future with more courage and optimism than remembering the glory moments, and everybody has a few of them."

A Feeling of Surprise

I WAS WALKING DOWN THE STREET WHEN I PASSED an antique store. Prominently displayed in the window was a *box camera*. An *antique*! Impossible! Why, that was the best camera I ever had and the only one I have ever been able to handle. What was it doing in that window?

My husband went back to speak to the psychology students at his alma mater, William and Mary College. He saw a glass cabinet in the hall containing various instruments. There was a sign on the window which said, "These instruments were used in the early days of psychology. Their use is unknown." My husband recognized everything on display very easily—they were the instruments used in his undergraduate psychology class.

Getting old is a great shock. The years have flown by, but inside our heads we still see ourselves the way we once were in the pictures in our albums. I see a picture of my husband with a wild shock of hair—how could it ever get gray and, even worse, begin to disappear? I see my high-school graduation picture and hardly recognize the wrinkled face in the mirror. It's all such a surprise. No matter how many old people we have known, when it happens to us it seems quite impossible.

Listening to two teenage girls on a bus one day, I heard one say to the other: "If I live until *forty*, I'll never get over this!" On a television talk show, I heard the host say, "Well, that's really something that pertains to old people, fifty on up." Who are these people talking about? ME—that's who. And the people in my life. I am surprised when my husband is stiff when he gets out of bed in the morning, and it hurts when he has to bend down. I am surprised when I pack for a trip that it takes me longer to pack the pills I might need than my clothes.

I try to remember how I once felt about people who were sixty-seven. When my parents were sixty-seven they didn't seem old to me because they were both still active and working. But when I was twenty-five or thirty I assumed they were over the hill already, so it seemed pretty good they were still ambulatory at sixty-seven! I thought my grandmother was a very old lady at sixty-three, but people looked much older at that age, then.

My picture of myself varies in relation to my daughter, between elation on the rare occasions when she says, "I'm calling for your advice," and the more common times when she sounds as if she'd feel better if I were safely put away in a nursing home.

What's the answer? Really very simple. I am not going to let a box camera, now an antique, or any thing or person tell me whether or not I am an antique. *I* will decide, and I'm not ready yet. My idea of an antique is that it has to be at least 150 years old, which gives me a little breather.

For All Those Born
Before 1930

SOONER OR LATER WE ARE MORE THAN LIKELY TO hear a someone, perhaps a grandchild, say, "You are so *old-fashioned*!" Nuts to that! I think there has never, ever been a generation more willing and able to roll with the punches of change than ours.

What made me think about this was an anonymous list of how our lives have changed sent to me by a doctor who sees many older patients—and is no spring chicken himself.* These are a few of the changes we sometimes forget and which we should tell our younger generations about.

For All Those Born Before 1930

We were born before television, penicillin, polio shots, frozen food, plastic, contact lenses, computers, and the Pill.

Before radar, credit cards, split atoms, pantyhose, dishwashers, air-conditioners, drip-dry clothes, and men walking on the moon.

*Courtesy of Marvin Meitus, M.D.

"Coming out of the closet" meant getting a piece of clothing, "designer jeans" meant a provocative girl named Jean, and "having a meaningful relationship" meant getting along well with our cousins.

"Fast food" meant it was Lent or Yom Kippur and "Outer Space" was the last two rows of a movie theater balcony.

There were no househusbands, computer dating, pornographic telephone numbers, day-care centers, electric typewriters, artificial hearts, or men wearing earrings (not since the time of pirates), and hardware was a store, not the opposite of software.

Things made in Japan were "junk," the five-and-ten-cent store sold things that were five and ten cents, a good car was about $600, and gas was eleven cents a gallon. A nickel got a Coke, an ice-cream cone, or a ride on the subway, and was enough to mail one letter and two postcards.

Cigarette smoking was glamorous, "grass" was what you mowed, "pot" was what you cooked in, and rock music was Grandma in a rocking chair singing a lullabye.

No instant coffee, no McDonald's, no cars with windows you couldn't roll down, no telephone-answering machines.

And, of course, we were the last generation that was dumb enough to think you needed a husband to have a baby or that parents should try to stick together for the sake of the children.

The list is endless, and we have adjusted brilliantly. But despite our courage, fortitude, and ingenuity, I keep getting these weird feelings that maybe we gave up and gave in too easily, on some counts.

Find Yourself a Carousel

ALL I WAS DOING, SITTING AT MY DESK, WAS PUSH-
ing papers around—getting more and more anxious
about the article and the two book outlines that were
past due. I felt tired and frustrated, and on top of everything else, it was a gorgeous day and I wanted to go out
for a walk.

After messing up page after page, I finally tore it all
up, threw it in the wastebasket, and decided there was
only one solution to my problem: I needed a ride on a
carousel. Fortunately for me, the carousel in Central
Park—the same one I've been riding for about sixty
years—is within walking distance.

It used to cost five cents a ride, and if you caught a
silver or a brass ring, there were extra rides. Now a
ticket is seventy-five cents with no free bonuses, but the
music is the same and the refurbished horses are wonderful. Soon I was sailing through the air, sciatica and
writing block forgotten.

I feel so close to my mother on a carousel; she died
almost seventeen years ago, but the stab of loneliness
and pain engulfs me for a moment. And then, I remem-

ber how I ran to the carousel, in grief and mourning when my darling friend Burr Tillstrom died, taking with him my dearest friends, Kukla and Ollie and Madame Oglepuss and Buelah Witch and all the other Kukla-politans who were such a joy for those of us old enough to remember the early days of television.

I felt such a mixture of joy and pain, as I rode my horse, round and round, exhilarated, delighted—*playful*. The joys of the past, the difficulties of the day, all meshed—a little girl allowing the real world to recede for something far more important and refreshing than sitting at my desk.

What happens, when I remember it is time for a carousel ride, is that when I become playful, the child inside me is allowed out for recess. A carousel makes me feel four years old again, and I am convinced that the only way to be creative and constructive in our adult years—especially the later ones—is to get back in touch with the child we once were.

It doesn't have to be a carousel for everyone. It might be fishing or a picnic or a game of miniature golf or going to a circus or anything else that takes us back in time and grants us a special, childlike freedom in which we accept all our thoughts and memories, sad and happy—and most of all, frees us from our grownup selves.

Many years ago, another darling friend, Fred Rogers, was out of his "Neighborhood" en route to a vacation and called me up in the midst of another writing crisis. I moaned and cried and said I was desperate, and I'd never finish the book. He was soothing and loving. "Oh,

Eda," he said, "you are a beautiful person and we all need you and love you." After about twenty minutes of tenderness, I hung up the phone, went to my typewriter, and it all became clear and possible. Then I did a double take. Why, that son of a gun was treating me like a four-year-old, I told myself.

Absolutely true and just what I needed. When we are tired or sad or truly grief-stricken over some terrible loss or find it impossible to do what we have to do, it is time to be playful, to comfort the inner child, to respect our need for nurturing. Find the place that can bring you to the lovely, special inner self that is with you from birth to death. It is the source of all creativity and of feeling most alive.

I patted my horse and said goodbye, went back to my desk, and went to work, refreshed, invigorated— *young*—knowing I could now do the work that needed to be done, until my next carousel ride.

Necessary Pilgrimages

THERE WAS AN ARTICLE IN A MAGAZINE A FEW YEARS ago about a ninety-year-old man, born to missionaries in China and living there for the first ten years of his life, who, despite opposition from his children, insisted that they join him on a pilgrimage to his past. Although his relatives thought he was probably senile, and several resented his spending hard-earned savings on such a "crazy trip" since they would have inherited the money when he died, there was no arguing with him. Off they went, searching out the grave of his father, meeting people who had heard of his parents from their parents, finding the place where the church had once stood before various revolutions. The old man seemed younger, had more energy, seemed happier than he'd been in years. Shortly after his return home, he died, a fulfilled man, first thanking his family for letting him complete his life's journey.

On a far less dramatic level, a few years ago my father (at about eighty-eight) asked me to take him to Brooklyn, to the place where his parents had lived, to say goodbye to two older, very ill sisters. Both sisters died shortly thereafter and I knew my father was reconciled because he had been able to say a last goodbye.

A few years ago Larry and I revisited the first place we'd lived, in Martinsburg, West Virginia, when he was in the army. Our memories were so nourishing—we had both been so young and yet we had worked so hard, accomplished so much in community service. It had been a promising beginning and we knew now it had borne rich fruit.

Every once in a while I get an urge to go and look at a Manhattan brownstone, at 147 West 153 Street. I lived there with my parents, grandparents, aunts, and uncles. My best friend, Janice, lived next door. Her father had died and this made me afraid. We played with dolls every day. Where there once was a yard, there now is a garage, but there was a special smell of weeds and earth and fruit trees that I could still sense, when I stood on the quiet street. The brownstone is now divided into separate apartments. I remember every room as it once was—and most of all I remember Grumpy, my grandfather's dog; I used to wheel him around in my doll carriage.

Why do we need to go back, to look back? A letter from an older woman tells of searching for information about her mother's family: "I knew nothing about her birthplace. . . . I found two living second cousins, one actually remembers my mother. . . ." There is a note of peace and fulfillment in the letter. There are necessary pilgrimages to places we have been, to places we feel connected to.

I think this need has to do with setting our lives

straight through knowing who we are, having an ever stronger sense of our own identity. We want to know who we really are, where we come from, what we have done with our lives. What it has to do with, I think, is that the most serene deaths, when they come, are to people who have no unfinished business.

We Raised
Ambassadors of Freedom

WHERE WERE YOU IN THE 1960S? RAISING FLOWER children? We had one. I recall the day I was standing in line at a movie theater and saw three girls approaching, all wearing red Columbia University nightgowns (and nothing else), walking barefoot on Broadway, probably the dirtiest street in the United States. At first I thought, "Thank God at least mine isn't that bad," and as they got closer, I saw our Wendy in the middle. All I thought about at the moment was the fact that I lived on the eleventh floor, and when I jumped it wouldn't hurt.

Oh, how scared we all were of our marvelous children! They were the pioneers of torn blue jeans and long-haired boys; we worried about girls taking the Pill—and even more about their not taking the Pill. We worried about jail for smoking marijuana. We were afraid they would get killed in antiwar demonstrations. And finally, if we had a brain in our heads, we began to realize how loving and unwarlike, how caring, they were—how *things* didn't matter to them. And then we saw them being mowed down by the Chicago police and killed at Kent State, and suddenly the whole country seemed to rise in wrath against these children, who, in truth, had listened to our moral lessons and who lived by them— the last thing we ever expected.

When my husband and I traveled in Europe, I admit we were sometimes uncomfortable and embarrassed. There were the dirty, unkempt American kids with their guitars—talking and singing, wherever they went, and by the 1980s most of them had been to every country they could visit and a few they weren't supposed to.

The first time I knew our children had been Johnny Appleseeds of democracy was when suddenly some of my friends who had children studying in Beijing were in terror as the Chinese students were run over by tanks and shot and beaten over the head. We worried and mourned for all, but there was a new awareness of the fact that American students were there among them. And when East Germany opened up, and Bulgaria and Hungary and Poland—and then Czechoslovakia—I remembered, suddenly and vividly, that wherever we traveled in the sixties and seventies there were always young Americans with bed rolls and knapsacks, behaving as if they had a right to be as individualistic as they wanted to be and taking freedom completely for granted.

Surely other factors were at work, mostly economic, and surely Walesa and Gorbachev, but the *hunger* for freedom one sees on the faces of the young men and women in these countries, so totally closed for so long, tells us that in some way, they've heard our kids. The seeds of freedom must have grown into a miraculous internal response, not only to leaders, not only to politics, not only to hunger and privation, but to a memory of our generation of children who took to the high seas and the low roads of the world (how nervous some of us were when they hit places we'd barely heard of) and left behind songs of freedom and the heady wine of a free society. What a generation! I feel so proud.

Our Personal Ghosts

WHEN I WAS A CHILD, THE WHITE SHEETS OF Halloween costumes both terrified and delighted me. After all, what did I know about ghosts? What do any children (or most, at least) know what older people like us know about the ghosts we carry inside us? You can't get to be sixty or sixty-five without knowing that ghost stories are not only those told in a group of happily shivering and shaking children, but another kind altogether.

Our ghost stories are all the people we have loved and lost. What we discover about aging is that if we stick around long enough, there are going to be an awful lot of ghosts. Most of all, for me, is my mother, who died about seventeen years ago. I wish she could see her great-grandchild. I understand the stresses and strains in her life, and I want to tell her I understand. I cherish a small book of poetry in which she wrote:

> Life, I challenge you to try me
> Doom me to unending pain . . .
> Thus I dare you; you can try me,
> Seek to make me cringe and moan,

Still my unbound soul defies you,
I'll withstand you—and alone!

How little I really knew and appreciated her courage. And then there is Aunt Lillie of the bell-like laugh, who would tell me endless stories and took me to my first movie at eight (*Sunny Side Up*) and loved me as if it were impossible to imagine me less than perfect, and Grandpa, who showed me faces in pansies, and Aunt Anne, who made a joke about everything and, under all the sharp wisecracks, was probably the kindest person I ever knew. And Norman, who opened me up to spontaneity and adventure, and oh, my darling friend Burr Tillstrom, who left and took Kukla and Ollie and Madame Oglepuss and Buelah Witch with him.

I once told a therapist that I could not bear all my losses, that they left me empty. And very wisely she said, "Eda, think how they have *filled* your life and left you a legacy of memories that will enrich your life for as long as you live."

How right she was. Each of us has grieved—and will do so often again—for the people we have loved and sometimes think we have lost. Until we are flooded with the sudden, sharp awareness that our lives would be so much less without our ghosts.

Mourning and celebration go hand in hand; the deeper our grief, the more there is for us to cling to, to rejoice about in memory. The ghosts in our lives are so often as real and as powerful as the living people around us. To lose someone we love is agony; to have had that love is a legacy precious beyond words.

Heavy thoughts on the edge of All Hallow's Eve—but not so inappropriate after all. When the doorbell rings on October 31, and we see before us two sparkling and mischievous eyes peering at us from under a sheet and a voice shouts, "Trick or treat!" as we hold out the bowl of fruits or nuts (we should know better than to encourage "a sugar high"!) what we might be thinking is that it's a good trick to love and be loved, and the treat is to remember the absolute reality of our personal ghosts and the gifts they gave us.

My Mother's Tree

I WATCHED WITH SOME TREPIDATION AS MY EIGHT-
year-old granddaughter tried to climb to the higher
branches of the red maple tree. "Look at me!" she
shouted. "Look how high I can go!" I started to tell her
to be careful and then, suddenly, I had the feeling that
she was very safe, in my mother's arms.

Seventeen years ago the tree was only about three
feet tall; now it is over twenty. It was planted when my
mother died, and her ashes were buried beneath the
tree. Our family and friends gathered in a circle, holding
hands around the tree, and a minister friend of ours read
a poem he had written about my mother. We hugged
and kissed and cried, and then we all had a wonderful
feast my daughter had prepared. Later we went to the
home of a friend who had a grand piano and another
friend, a concert pianist, played for us.

And now, a little girl my mother would have loved
was climbing the branches of the tree, and I felt such a
sense of her great-grandmother's presence. My daughter
calls the tree "Gran-Jean's Tree," since that was what
my daughter called her grandmother. The tree will be

there for as far ahead in time as I can imagine, and hopefully future generations of children will also be enfolded in my mother's arms.

Whatever our unique and special religious beliefs may be—whether we perceive of death as the beginning of another existence, or whether we don't—there is, I think, a universal truth we can all share, and that is that there can be a very special joy in living memorials.

A friend who was a social worker left a grant, in her name, to a social agency that is devoted to service to the elderly homeless. A woman I know who did not have the financial resources to leave any money, but who was a gourmet cook, got herself several hundred 3 x 5 file cards and four index boxes the year before she died and wrote out her recipes for her four grand-children. How often they must remember her, in their kitchens, when company is coming!

Each of us has special talents, ideas, feelings, and acts by which we can be remembered: in a hand-crocheted afghan, in our photograph albums of the history of our family, in a sketch we made, in a composition we once wrote about a camping trip. Our children and grandchildren, our nieces and nephews, our close (and younger!) friends might be greatly comforted in the grief of missing us, if we have left some tangible message behind.

Each of us needs to feel we have in some way changed the world for the better during our lifetime: raised some decent kids, been kind to our parents, helped neighbors and friends, contributed in some way to our community. As well as any other kind of immortality we may believe in, I think there is a natural and universal wish to leave earthly messages about the meaning and purpose of our lives.

As I watched my darling little granddaughter exulting at having reached a branch so high that she shouted, "Grandma, I can see the *world*!" it reminded me that for the rest of the days of my life, I wanted to express my own personal message to the world: that love is the most important ingredient in living, that children are our greatest treasure, that all human beings all over the world need and deserve the same opportunities for the fullest use of their abilities, and that this planet, the only one we know, must be treasured and not defiled.

When my grandchild returned to earth, I knew my messages to her would be loud and clear in the books I'd written for children—maybe later, in the ones for grownups, too. What we leave behind may be helpful to those we love, and maybe even more important in helping us face our own mortality.

Telling It Like It Was

MY HUSBAND AND I WERE SITTING IN A RESTAU-
rant in our neighborhood having lunch. Much fuss was
being made by the waiters after about fifteen people
came in together, and we heard them saying the name
of the bank around the corner from which they had
come. We recognized a few of the tellers and executives.
We figured that maybe this new restaurant had gotten
a loan from the bank in order to get started, but what
held our attention was the makeup of these congenial,
affectionate men and women—blacks, Hispanics, and
whites.

They were all too young to marvel at what knocked
us out: they were apparently color- and ethnic-blind.
Their ease could not be faked.

In about 1941 and 1942, I worked with a wonderful
religious and community leader, Algernon Black, who
was surely partly responsible for the anti-discrimination
laws of New York, and we members of his committee
were trying to integrate the work force at Macy's and
Nedicks. It was one helluva fight. In my childhood all
black people in the movies were either maids or enter-

tainers; people thought Stepin Fetchit was funny, when he was really a symbol of how to handle rage without getting shot. I listened to Billie Holiday singing "Strange Fruit," all about lynchings. There were one or two "Negroes" in each class in my private progressive school—our token obeisance to liberalism. When my family went on vacation in the South, and my brother saw benches designated "colored" and "white," he asked in amazement, "Who thought *that* up?" But in the North almost every black woman he ever saw was taking care of a white child. When the one token black in my class was invited to a birthday party on Park Avenue, her mother had to bring her through the service entrance of the building. And watching sports events on TV, I can remember when Jackie Robinson stood *entirely* alone.

Many of my life experiences during sixty-seven years have been as a part of the struggle for change, but somehow I didn't think I'd live long enough to see the camaraderie I now see in department stores and offices. I recently went to Alabama—Montgomery, no less—to a women's prison, and when I mentioned to the warden that I couldn't believe my eyes, seeing the prison so thoroughly integrated at every level, she looked at me blankly, as if I were weird; was she too young to remember the Selma March and the unintegrated institutions, from schools to buses to Woolworth's lunch counters? Could she not have seen those brave little children in Little Rock, Arkansas, being led into school by Federal troops?

We still see rage among blacks—and justifiably, because the job isn't done. We see insensitivity on the part of many whites—but, my God, what miracles have happened in a few decades of the twentieth century! Every time I see a black lawyer or doctor on television, I am still overcome by excitement and thanksgiving, and I think we need to tell younger people about history and the human capacity to change, even if too slowly for many. It is still a miracle, a triumph, to those of us old enough to remember when we gave so little thought to blacks that they weren't even regarded as second-class citizens!

There are hundreds of issues about which younger people have no historical perspective—and we are the generation that can give it to them. Our children think we're neurotic when we carry on because a grandchild has a fever of 104°. They know an antibiotic will bring it down in a day. We remember the terror, the crises, and the deaths caused by diphtheria, scarlet fever, and smallpox.

I recently wrote an article in which I mentioned that my family and the doctor became terror-stricken when they asked my younger brother if he could bend his neck and he couldn't. A young editor called and said, "Eda, I didn't understand that part about bending the neck. Why was everyone so upset?" Imagine! Being so young she'd never heard about a common diagnostic procedure for polio!

Young people don't remember a world in which men held doors open for ladies and people wrote thank-you letters and the only medicines for the flu were aspirin and Argyrol (they've never heard of that, I'm sure). They don't remember a world we lived in or heard about—

my father slept in a bed with five relatives; his sisters, in their early teens, worked twelve to fourteen hours a day, six days a week; City College was free; and he walked back and forth every day (about six miles) because he didn't have any carfare.

So many changes! Personal, social, medical customs and rules; and for those younger than we, there are only a limited number of living historians who didn't study history but lived it. We need to tell it like it was.

The Many Faces
of Friendship

SOMETIMES I THINK WE GET CAUGHT IN A TRAP when we think about friendship. The idea becomes stereotyped: a friend is someone we know a long time and see often. Not necessarily so.

On a trip to Europe, attending a conference at which my husband spoke, I met a woman who thought his speech was as magnificent as I did. I had never met her before but already we had a common thread of understanding and appreciation! We saw a lot of each other in the following four days and it was perfectly clear by the time we parted that we liked each other a lot, that we would see each other again. We even talked about personal matters that we hadn't shared with people we'd known for years.

The day we returned from this trip I discovered that one of my dearest friends had a fatal illness. *We had met only once.* But she, like me, wrote articles for *Woman's Day* and by writing fan letters to each other we became a mutual admiration society. For a number of years we shared our deepest thoughts and feelings by mail, and we got to know each other through the books we had written. We met once in a television studio in Toronto and it was as if we had known each other all our lives. Her writing was filled with insight, love, a passion for life, which flowed through her work with such warmth and vitality that anyone reading it had to feel they knew her. My ninety-three-year-old father was so moved by one of her stories that he wrote to tell her that a lullaby she'd mentioned was the one his mother sang to him as a little boy in Russia almost one hundred years ago.

On a hurried, hectic, busy short trip to New York from Canada, my "pen pal" went to visit my father (I was out of town). I can count on the fingers of one hand the number of my friends, living right nearby, who have visited him. But she understood how she had spoken to his heart and how he saw her as a daughter. When she dies (she has terminal cancer) I will have lost one of my dearest friends—based only on the articles and books and letters we shared.

A friend can be someone you have known all your life or someone you met a week ago—or someone you never met except through a book or a beautiful movie or a play or a piece of music or a painting. Or someone who has served as a role model and made you proud to be a fellow human being. My friends include Monet and Mozart, Arthur Miller and Arthur Laurents, Federico Fellini and Thomas Wolfe, Louisa May Alcott and Eleanor Roosevelt, and a hundred other human beings who have lifted my spirits and made me more than I was before they touched my life. They remind me that friendship is the source of love and growth, whatever form it may take.

When Relationships End

M Y FRIEND BETTY CAME FOR LUNCH RECENTLY. We hadn't even seen each other for several years. She's bright and funny and leads a fascinating and glamorous life, and I looked forward so much to seeing her. Unfortunately she was almost completely preoccupied with one subject—the fact that a close friendship of thirty years seemed to be in trouble. We spent most of our time together discussing what could have happened, who got mad at whom, what might be some hidden agenda, which of several events might have precipitated the loss of connection and affection.

Finally—I was a little slow that day—I asked, "Do you still really like these people? Do you still have a lot in common? Do you feel lost without them?" Betty was thoughtful for a moment and then she said, "Hell, no, to all those questions! They bore me. I've changed a lot and they haven't." There was a startled look in her big, beautiful blue eyes. We both laughed and I told her I would not charge her for this consultation since it was too easy!

All of us hang on to some relationships long past the

time they have real meaning in our lives. We forget that if we are truly alive we are constantly changing, and while some wonderful friendships endure because both parties are growing and changing, this is not always the case. I have a friend in California—we have known each other since first grade over sixty years ago, and when we meet after a year or two, we can pick up exactly where we now are because we are both growing and changing in similar ways. On the other hand, there was another girl in that same first-grade class whom I hung on to for dear life long after I knew our values were at the opposite ends of the world. I hung on despite hating the way she talked about people she considered beneath her social level, or the way she lavished the most excessive luxuries on herself, because there was also this sixty-year history. It's not really so simple and that's why it hurts. It wasn't just the sixty-year history that held us together too long; it was that, like sisters, we had had many shared joys and times of great affection and mutual understanding. The problem is whether history and good and bad times, when weighed in the balance, mean sticking with each other or letting go. In Betty's case she faced her boredom; in my case finally there was an episode I could not tolerate—debts she refused to honor despite the real needs of the lenders.

In my life there have been four or five women friends whom I still miss often, ever since one or the other of us ended the relationship. A talented artist I met in college and at long years of family gatherings; a colleague whom I loved and respected, who suddenly attacked me in public; a woman who didn't seem to be growing or

changing at all, so when she acted like forty at the age
of sixty, we couldn't connect anymore.

Rather than dwelling endlessly on "what's happening"
when a relationship seems to be dying, we need to take
an honest look and then accept that something that was
once good isn't anymore.

The nice part is that in the last ten years I have made
new friends who are so exciting, so talented, so em-
pathic, so caring, that I still get the nourishment I need
from friendship and can give it back as well.

Old Friendships

DOROTHY, BARBARA, AND I HAD A DATE. WE WERE going to have lunch and go to a matinée. You find nothing remarkable about that? You are right, of course— friends meet for dates frequently. What is remarkable about this is that we three hadn't seen each other since the 1940s. I couldn't imagine what it would be like, but we had been talking on the phone and it felt as if we had never separated.

We belonged to a teenage club during World War II. Not too many fellas around, and in those days girls hadn't yet realized how much fun they could have without male companionship. Come to think of it, we may have been ahead of our time, because we *did* have some great times together. We invited an Australian sailor, through the USO, to go on a country picnic with us and we all laughed bravely all day, even though we knew he was going back to the war in the Pacific. We walked all over New York, often getting home at two in the morning, without ever wondering if we were in danger (we weren't). We went to meetings where we earnestly and seriously talked about how we wanted the world to be after the war.

Dorothy brought us closest, personally, to a war we couldn't even imagine when she met and married a refugee who had escaped the ovens of Europe. It was too much to believe. Barbara married a man we all knew and I met a skinny soldier; we were married after spending less than three weeks together—one of those war romances that can't last. Our forty-fifth anniversary tended to disprove our rash decision. Barbara was the first person I told about our engagement. She visited us a few times at Larry's post in West Virginia, where he and I, not realizing we could be lynched, were starting an interracial council. The townspeople asked the army to move my husband to another post but to the captain's everlasting credit he refused and the army psychiatrist came to our next meeting to talk about "The Roots of Prejudice."

After the war we all lived some distance from each other. Because he thought he was just joining some club (the reserves!), my husband was called back for the Korean War. There has now been one divorce, one death, one remarriage, a collection of children and grandchildren. I don't even remember who made the first move—I think it was Dorothy. Over the phone we all brought each other up to date. We felt as if we were twenty and no time had intervened.

If you want to feel young again and get a breath of fresh air, there is nothing like turning the clock back and looking for old kid pals. Lots of times it will be a bust; I re-met one woman I knew long ago and we couldn't stand each other. But it is worth the experiment. I suspect there is something very, very special about those early ties that will refresh the soul. I'll keep you informed!

Remembering Loved Ones

M Y MOTHER DIED SEVENTEEN YEARS AGO. MY FA-
ther gave me all her file folders—she had extensive files
on her work, which was in much the same field as mine—
and slowly over the years I have discarded her notes,
painfully, but knowing my poor daughter will have
enough to contend with, sorting all my stuff when I die.
The other day I started to use one of the folders and
found this list on a piece of yellowing paper:

TITLE IDEA, "FILE UNDER 'SOMEDAY' "

Things I would like to do, and wonder if ever
someday!
  Fix my scrap books, photo albums, and loose
    photos.
  Throw out old letters, pamphlets, notes for
    speeches, etc.
  Fix files.
  Throw out things in closets we don't need.
  Answer correspondence.
  Write articles and stories.
  Invite old friends.
  Convince Max we should take more trips while
    we can still walk,
  Etc., etc.

It is a list I could have written yesterday, today, or tomorrow. I have two closets and an old army footlocker from World War II filled with letters and pictures crying out for some organization. I know the feeling behind making such a list—a kind of scream in the dark to make order out of the chaos of a long and busy life. I feel glad that she talked my father into lots of trips before she died and before he stopped walking. I look down at my hands as I type this and see her hands; I look in the mirror and I see her face; when I give a lecture and tell a lot of stories, I'm doing what she did until she died at seventy-eight.

For each of us there are daily reminders of the people we loved who have died. They didn't "pass away," they died. Any attempt to sugarcoat that fact takes something away from one's memories, which can be so strong, so poignant—and so life-enhancing. The only way I can deal with the death of loved ones is to know that each person, so special, so different, lives on in me—what I remember, what I do that is something they would have done or felt. Not slavishly—not denying my own uniqueness—but enriching my life by adding something of each person to my own nature.

I know people who would have come across a note in a file the way I did, and would have cried and torn it to shreds and thrown it away—as if that would end the pain. Not me. I cried—and then I told you about my mother.

The Circle of Caring

MY FATHER, AT NINETY-FOUR, HAD ONE CLASS-mate still alive from his college days. When I heard Harry had died, I felt some anxiety about telling my father. What astounded me was that he hardly reacted at all. His explanation of his feelings moved me very much and, I think, gave me a new insight about the feelings of people over the age of ninety.

He said, "You must wonder why I am not more upset. But I have reached an age when the circle of caring has grown very small. Almost all my friends and relatives have died. Death is the next step for me as well. It is no longer possible to make a connection with many people. As one gets older and older the connections to life become one's children and grandchildren. There is a sense of preparation for one's own leaving the world."

Now I could understand many things that I could not yet experience myself; my father had puzzled me since my mother's death eighteen years ago. He had always been a very social, active, caring person. He and my mother had at least one hundred intimate friends! I knew that my mother had been the organizer of their social life, but when she died, I thought he would be eager to see his close friends and relatives. With some pushing on my part, he did see or call people and was visited from time to time, but without any apparent relish. He was reluctant to meet new people, refused to join any groups, remained contented, it seemed, to be alone much of the time. I was puzzled; this wasn't at all like the father I knew as a child.

Now that I see the same pattern developing in myself I am beginning to understand—and his explanation has helped to clarify what is happening. I too had a rich and active social life when I was younger. In our thirties and forties, we and most of our contemporaries met at dinner parties, went to the theater together, talked on the phone frequently—often about our problems as parents. Slowly but surely life has changed. No more dinner parties, much greater selectivity in choosing people we want to maintain a relationship with, closer contacts with new people whom we don't see very often but correspond with. I often think and wonder about all the relationships that were once strong and intense but sort of drifted away as we got older.

By the time we are sixty, I think we are just beginning to move toward a much smaller circle of caring. We get tired more easily, we find traveling difficult—we go to bed earlier! By the time we are in our eighties and nineties the circle of caring will narrow even more. As we move toward death there is a kind of stripping away of non-essentials—both things and people—a kind of psychic readiness for the ultimate aloneness of death. It is not tragic or neurotic behavior, but rather the beginning of readiness to move out of the here and now and into a reality beyond understanding. The closing circle of caring means that one's goodbyes will be to those who always remain the most significant—children, grandchildren, perhaps a sibling or an old friend. We are learning to live with loss by closing the circle of caring.

Happy Old *Years*

THE OLDER I GET THE MORE I AM CONVINCED THAT the best way to spend New Year's Eve is to remember years gone by—special memories, echoes, and shadows. Nothing can help us face the unknown future with more courage and optimism than remembering the glory moments, and everybody has a few of them.

This New Year's Eve these are some of the things I think I'll remember. I may change my mind and decide on a different selection—that doesn't matter; it's a feeling of the treasures we bring with us into the next year.

I remember the first date I had with my husband, Larry. It was in Kansas City and he was a soldier, and I knew he was the most attractive young man I'd ever met and that we could talk to each other for fifty years and never get bored. (Boy, was I right!)

I remember the day our grownup daughter, unasked, volunteered, "God, when I get to know other people's parents, I sure do appreciate you two!"

I remember my (then) son-in-law coming out of the delivery room in a green smock holding my granddaughter a few minutes after she was born.

I remember going to the theater with my mother and

our holding hands as the lights went down and it was "magic time" for both of us. I remember refusing to leave the theater after seeing Katharine Cornell in *Romeo and Juliet* because nothing would ever be as wonderful in real life.

Thank goodness this is written for the "over sixties" so I don't have to explain who Burr Tillstrom was, or his "Kukla, Fran, and Ollie." One of the luckiest things that ever happened to me is that we became friends, and among other joys, I performed with Kukla and Ollie and Madame Oglepuss and Buelah Witch and Fletcher Rabbit in Chicago. And once, sitting next to Burr in the basement of Fran Allison's home in New Jersey, we held hands watching all the kinescopes of the 1950s. I miss Burr and Fran, but the fact that Ollie and Kukla died with him is more than I can bear—but how lucky I was.

I remember almost fainting with joy when at a seacoast town in England we came upon the bookshop of the *real* Christopher Robin. I remember the thrill of seeing the first thatched roof in France. I remember my father reading me poetry on a park bench when I was recovering from chicken pox. On and on, the memories flood forth.

I remember an award luncheon at Columbia Teachers College, and I remember an Emmy nomination for my TV program, "How Do Your Children Grow?" and the day my husband gave a magnificent speech at a conference in Holland. I remember my daughter, so tender and caring, working with retarded children—oh, so many memories to savor. Look back before you look forward. Happy New Year!

III

GROWING
AND
CHANGING

"It is natural to be curious about the future—to wish we knew some answers to current questions—but I try not to think about it all too much, to just live long enough to be useful and loving, and hope that somewhere along the way there will be some meaning in my having lived."

Taking Risks

THIS IS THE SCENE: MY HUSBAND LARRY AND I ARE sitting in an off-Broadway theater watching a charming and delightful musical, having a perfectly wonderful time because up on the stage there happens to be a gentleman who has had his Social Security card for several years and who is cavorting joyously—singing, dancing, acting his heart out. He happens to be a dear friend, Dave, who always wanted to be an actor but thought it would also be nice to have a wife and children, and, in the absence of a national theater to help him remain employed, spent thirty years in the news department of a major television station.

When he retired several years ago, he started taking tap dance and singing lessons; he went to every audition, commercial and theatrical, calling for men slightly long in the tooth—but a remarkable thing happened: he got so happy, doing what he had always longed to do, that he began looking ten, fifteen years younger. When a bus driver asked to see his Medicare card, Dave said, "I could kiss you!"

He'd been in a number of traveling companies and

now he was off-Broadway. Watching him onstage gave us a natural high. Here was the perfect role model for anyone in their sixties and older. If you want something badly enough, and have the courage to take enormous risks, anything is possible. We were watching a man who doesn't have time to worry about getting older.

Some of us will take enormous risks, others less dramatic ones. For example, my idea of a risk is to continue to travel, while packing a heating pad and a bag of pills for my arthritic bones. I know a woman who took a big risk and started law school at fifty-seven; I know a man who took a smaller risk and, widowed, sold his city apartment and went to live in a tiny cabin in the Vermont woods. A woman in a wheelchair who goes shopping by herself at a supermarket is a risk-taker.

There is a catch in all this if one is married. When we hugged our friend Dave and blessed him for his courage (and the talent it would have been death to hide), he said, "More than fifty percent of all this belongs to Millie." His wife and I met in first grade and have been friends for about sixty years. So it did not come as any great surprise to me that despite very real hazards and difficulties it created in her life, she was totally gung ho about the birth of a sixty-plus actor. A theater buff herself, it wasn't only "go, boy, go," but time and counsel and total commitment.

It's very hard to take little or big risks as we get older unless somebody is there to push a little as well as pick up the pieces when there are inevitable failures. How often did we—do we—say, "Don't be an idiot, it's too late to do that," or "We're too old to adjust to having less money," or "The children will think you are crazy"?

When we are lucky enough to find a couple in the act of reaffirming themselves and life, it is balm for our aging souls. I want all of us to some way, somehow, look as exultant as our friend did, up on that stage.

It's very nice to have a support system when we want or need to take risks. But many older people don't have a partnership because of divorce or widowhood or a long-term single life. That doesn't mean that greater and smaller risks are not possible. What it means is that we may turn to grown children, friends, and relatives to cheer us on from the bleachers. But even braver are the people who will have to make the choice to test themselves really alone, or perhaps with the help of a therapist or counselor.

It's happening every day: a cancer patient, diagnosed as terminal, who decides to "blow it all" and take a trip around the world; a ninety-year-old man who arranges to go to a camp for poor kids to play Grandpa; a sixty-year-old secretary who decides to go to computer school before she's forced to retire. It's probably harder to take risks without a chorus of well-wishers behind us, but it is possible to be one's own cheerleader. Either way, by the time we are in our sixties our "biological clocks" are ticking, and there is no time to waste before the birth of our truest selves.

The Health Cult

WHEN I WAS A YOUNG WOMAN I FELT GUILTY BE-
cause I wasn't a perfect parent. By middle age I felt
guilty to discover I did not have a perfect marriage.
Now, in my sixties, I feel terribly guilty because I don't
jog around Central Park every morning.

We all know about the Youth Cult—the feeling that
if we are old we are barely tolerated by society, that fat
and old are absolute no-nos in this culture. Now it
seems to me we have to add the Health Cult. I can
hardly bear to talk about it, I'm so ashamed. If it weren't
considered a sin of major proportions, I would hereby
admit, but not easily, that my idea of exercise is getting
out of bed in the morning and walking into the kitchen
to make breakfast.

But, I hasten to add, I try hard to be an acceptable
member of society at least in this regard: I swim every
chance I get (if I can find a pool with 83° water) and
I walk as much as my arthritic feet will allow. I do
not doubt for one moment that the jogging-running-
aerobics crowd is absolutely right and will outlive me.
I passionately admire those who play tennis at ninety.

I've never met a doctor who didn't tell me to *move*, as quickly and as much as possible.

But at least let me confess, at long last—the burden is too heavy for me to carry alone any longer—that in my fantasy life I am permanently lying on a chaise lounge being fed hot chocolate by a charming French maid in a black satin uniform with white frills. There are other fantasies, but they are too shameful to mention even in a confession like this. I know that exercise is the road to a longer and healthier life, and I try to heed all the warnings about what happens to people like me who would rather sit or lie down most of the time.

The biggest problem is to recognize that eating properly and exercising sensibly is different from fasting two days a week and eating alfalfa the rest of the time; it is different from jogging on city streets two hours a day, on cement, and breathing in all the car fumes along the way. What it is, really, is facing up to the fact that when we were children we had a dessert every day (unless we were being punished), at two meals at least, that if we had enough money we felt very lucky to eat steaks and chops almost every day—and that most of the adults around us were far more interested in our exercising our brains than our bodies. If we want to feel good and live, we have to knock out everything we were taught in the good old days when fried chicken and smoking were considered okay. It's a tough struggle—let no one underestimate it. I guess I'll go walk around the block— fast enough to improve my cardiovascular system, as my daughter told me I must do.

Saving and Spending

I RECENTLY RECEIVED A LETTER WHICH REPORTED that the writer knew a man who lived in relative poverty until he died and it was then discovered that he had left an estate worth three million dollars. That is, of course, carrying the fear of dependency to a ridiculous extreme. On the other hand, I know a lawyer who surely should have known better, who was always so generous to everyone, made no plans for living a long life, and in his nineties is entirely dependent on a Social Security check that covers less than a third of his monthly expenses. There are people who have more stocks and bonds and insurance policies than they could use up in three lifetimes, and there are others who "forget" to maintain their health-insurance payments.

Somewhere there must be a better balance. A widow wrote me that she and her husband had been saving to take an around-the-world cruise for twenty years, and he died two months before they were to leave. Needless to say she felt bitter and miserable about all the pleasures they had had to forgo to save that much money. There is no possible way in which we can perfectly plan for the future—there will always be unexpected events and mitigating circumstances. But we need to strive for some middle-of-the-road philosophy. We need to plan for the realities of life as best we can, but we also ought to feel that it is equally important to be helpful to others while we can, to support good causes we believe in, and certainly to have some fun and recreation. Probably the best way to work out a sensible balance between spending and saving is to discuss such matters with experts—and to be very sure the people we choose to consult are well known, have a reputation for ethical services, and don't promise to make us millions if we only invest in some new gold mine in Zanzibar. (That is just an expression—I don't know anything about Zanzibar!) We need to talk to sensible, responsible people, highly recommended by other sensible, reliable people. Then we have to decide on our own unique and special values and goals. I don't want to have a penniless old age, but on the other hand, I would rather give some of my worldly goods to my daughter while I'm alive so I can share in the pleasures of her life. My husband and I took our first trip to Europe when our combined income was $12,000 a year, and our friends thought we were out of our minds. We borrowed money and spent a long time paying it back. But when we go to Europe now—often for speaking engagements—I am *so glad* we didn't wait. At that time every place we went was beautiful and thrilling; now the cities are dirty, expensive, noisy, crowded, and exactly like staying home.

I don't think it's wise to put off too many pleasures for too long nor do I want to worry so much about the future that I withhold help from those I love, or stop contributing to good causes, especially those with concern for saving this planet. The balance between foolish and hazardous spending and becoming a year-round Scrooge is not easy.

I must admit that I tend toward making sure one's current life is adventurous and rich. I'm especially fond of a cartoon picturing a lawyer's office in which the lawyer is reading a will to the family: "Being of sound mind and disposition, I blew it all!"

The Dead Weight
of Big Lies

A FRIEND SENT ME A MAGAZINE ARTICLE ABOUT A very famous mutual friend. The article was about this woman, her husband, her marriage, and her children. The article arrived with a note: "Did we ever meet this woman???"

The article, "as told to" a reporter, described a perfect marriage, a blissful life, and wonderful children. It never occurred to me that the reporter had embellished the story; I knew it was exactly as told. It described a life of wonderful adventures; it described a genius husband and the fulfilling, creative life of the wife, and listed the accomplishments of children who had grown up in the limelight.

What I knew, beyond a shadow of doubt, was that the genius husband was often abusive and had had numerous affairs. I knew that his wife suffered from periodic depressions but had refused treatment. I knew that the son, although a successful Wall Street broker, was an alcoholic and the daughter had made a disastrous marriage at sixteen.

I have changed the facts slightly, but when I saw the magazine article I had a visual image of a woman carrying a dead weight—maybe a ton or two—on her fragile back, trying desperately to maintain the illusion of perfection in the face of normal human vulnerability and some very serious problems. What a load! What a burden! Many of the family's problems were surely exacerbated by maintaining the myths.

It is not only the rich and famous who carry such burdens. We all do it to some degree and there is no question it can cause fatigue and loneliness. Some things we keep to ourselves because we don't want to hurt someone else; we accept the fact that some lies—or at least evasions—are simply good manners and a sign of caring. We have been taught not to "wash dirty linen in public." But it seems to me that in the last twenty-five years or so people in all generations are learning that "telling it like it is" can be very comforting and that the support of other people in very similar circumstances is extremely therapeutic. Alcoholics Anonymous, Parents Without Partners, widows and widowers, people who can't lose weight, and cancer support groups have all discovered the solace and inspiration of sharing their honest woes.

The same thing is happening with older people, but there may be more reluctance among us over-sixties. We were probably taught as children to keep family secrets, not to talk about our troubles. Few people were admitting to the normal problems of being human.

I am encouraged by news, for example, of senior citizen centers now providing group counseling where older people can share their hurts, disappointments, and anxieties, as well as their anger. Hospitals, nursing homes, and convalescent centers are all discovering that what's good for younger generations is good for us. The first step in unloading a weight of lies is to feel good enough about oneself not to feel shame, not to feel guilty and responsible for human failures, for human pain. We can't share our burden of lies until we recognize that every single person we know is carrying a similar load.

When we were children we were taught to share our toys. Now we have to learn to share our humanity so we can stand up straighter.

One Person
Makes a Difference

Author Jo Coudert, whom I have loved for many years because of her fantastic book *Advice From a Failure*,* wrote an article for *Woman's Day* (December 19, 1989) called "I'm a Bag Lady for the World." In it she tells of loving to take walks in the semi-rural area where she lives but finding it essential, despite its interfering with a beloved activity, to stop along the way and pick up other people's garbage.

She and I are soulmates. When I had a house on Cape Cod I took a plastic bag with me whenever I went for a walk, and collected beer cans, soda bottles, and McDonald's wrappings along the way. I was furious at the people who had so little concern for their planet but I figured bending so much was good for me. Ms. Coudert decided more recently that she would become "a fool for the world." She writes, "We've finally come to understand that the world is our home—that an oil spill thousands of miles away is in our front yards, that the

---

*Scarborough House (1983).

greenhouse effect warms us all, that it is our water being polluted, our food adulterated. . . . We also feel helpless to do much about it." She quotes Shirley Temple Black (that adorable curly-head has turned out pretty well!), who said, "Think globally, act locally."

I get a lot of sad mail from people who are handicapped by old age or specific disabilities. They say that their lives are useless and meaningless, that they have nothing to do. Others, healthy and whole, write of loneliness, of not feeling needed by grown children.

In the city of New York, I feel essential at least to my neighborhood because I pick up all the garbage I pass and take it to the next trash can I pass. I write furious letters to congressmen and department heads about black smoke coming out of chimneys and places where the Sanitation Department doesn't go because the people are too poor and discouraged to fight City Hall.

We have no business complaining that we are not useful and that nobody needs us. The world needs every ounce of strength left in our bodies to fight the disasters we could never have imagined when we were young.

Many of the young activists of the sixties became very discouraged about not having the power to change society; I, however, feel they did PLENTY by helping to end a terrible war. However, now what many of those "flower children" in their late thirties and forties say is that they have learned the power of individual action. A Wall Street banker gives two evenings a week working in a shelter for the homeless; two young women walk the streets of their town with hot coffee and sandwiches for families sleeping in cars and people hidden in the shadows of store entrances. One young woman organized a letter campaign for better streetlights and got them.

Old age is no excuse for copping out. Each of us can find ways in which to make a difference. I got a letter from the daughter of a woman with terminal cancer who had inserted a letter in her will that she did not want life-support systems used when her life as a real person was over. Several months before she died, she told her daughter, "Listen, just before you pull the plug, I want you to send this money to Greenpeace in my memory," and handed her daughter a fifty-dollar bill.

How to Survive the News

SEVERAL YEARS AGO, FOR THE FIRST OF THREE TIMES, I saw the British musical *Me and My Girl* in London. I loved it so much I saw it twice more in New York, but despite its being delightful, silly, and funny, I cried every time. Insanity? I like to think not. I cried most of all in London because I knew that this light-hearted show had first been performed during the London Blitz; I knew that the performers and the soldiers, sailors, and civilians in the audience, laughing and singing, knew that at any moment the theater could be bombed and they would all die. I felt overwhelmed by that capacity for courage and wasn't at all sure I could have measured up. I had heard "The Lambeth Walk" as a teenager, three thousand miles from the danger.

I was playing the record of the show the other day, just before turning on the evening news. It came to me as a sudden, shocking insight that I—all of us—are in even more danger now than those wartime audiences in Great Britain. The Second World War may have wiped out millions of people, but *the planet survived*. None of us can now be sure we will be so lucky. The 1989 summer heat—it followed me to England and followed me back home—was frightening. We wonder if the poisons we are creating are changing our environment. I watch a program which tells me that fish are dying all over the world from asphyxiation—not enough oxygen. A little more of this, and *we* won't be able to breathe. There was a report of a family being evacuated from a town after it was learned the houses had been built over a toxic dump; they had moved from Love Canal. My granddaughter calls and says, "Grandma, don't eat any more tuna fish. They catch them in big nets and kill dolphins." I remember Venice as one of the most romantic and beautiful cities I'd ever seen, and now, on the television news, I watch people pushing away the slime of algae along the entire Italian coast. I see that nobody in this entire country is prepared to give up driving a car to work and take a train instead, even if it means death to the world. A commentator warns that if we don't stop breathing because of the ocean pollution, we will stop when they cut down the last trees in the forests of South America.

I realize it isn't necessarily bravery that keeps us going, but massive denial of the dangers. We don't really believe in our own mortality any more than we believe the planet could die. We sing and dance and try not to think about it; we talk worriedly but we do not make the massive demands of our world leaders to save us that are desperately needed.

I, for one, plan to give as much money as I possibly can to organizations like Greenpeace. I will vote only for political leaders who are willing to face the fact that overpopulation is the most serious problem of all and will take drastic measures to deal with this. It's brave to face death, but it is much more courageous to fight for life. My granddaughter at eight is learning about ecology in second grade. Our only real hope is a new generation ready to pay the price for survival.

Plant a Tree

About twenty years ago my husband and I went to visit a Methodist minister who so well understood the fundamental principles of his religion that, while leading a suburban church, he spent all the parishioners' money on helping those in trouble and other good works. Naturally he was fired, and he decided to move to the upper reaches of Vermont, where he bought an old farm with lots of land and became an itinerant preacher—all over the world. He is a dear friend, and twenty years ago he took us to see an area where he had planted hundreds of tiny fir trees—just seedlings, then.

I have just returned from another visit and my breath was taken away when I viewed a forest of trees, each one easily thirty or more feet high. What a joy to see the fruition of this man's dream.

Sometime ago President Bush made a speech about each person planting a tree and I thought it was, to say the least, an inadequate response to the loss of Brazilian forests and the greenhouse effect, but I've changed my mind. The thing about my friend's forest is not only that he planted and planned for the future, but that he is a man who now feels a profound sense of being a part of the land, even an important citizen of the planet.

For those of us over sixty, chances are we would be able to see a tree grow for another twenty years, and even if we didn't we would know it was there. If ever there was a world that needed replenishing of natural resources, this is surely IT. The older we get the more I think we need to feel that we are leaving good works behind us.

I don't think I will ever recover from the fact that after we moved from a home in New Jersey, the young couple who bought our house cut down every tree we had planted, all growing under our tender and loving care for five years. But after my visit to Vermont it occurred to me that there is still time. What those of us who live in apartment houses can do is to offer to plant a tree on the grounds if there are any. An alternative would be to call the local Parks Department and offer to pay for a planting.

Aside from helping to save the planet I think planting trees is a fine metaphor for what to do about getting old. Instead of sitting and wringing our hands because so much of our lives is behind us, we need to think creatively about what we can do for the future. And in this ailing world the opportunities are endless. A wonderful cure for "the old-age blues" is to ask: "What can I do for future generations?" It would be impossible to run out of possibilities during the rest of our lives.

A New Life—As a Volunteer

MANY MONTHS AGO I WROTE ABOUT THE OPPOR-
tunities available to older people to volunteer their services in many a good cause. I received a letter in which
I was told in no uncertain terms that I was a naive romantic at best, that volunteers were exploited, that they
were only given the most menial tasks and were "treated
like dirt." I knew this wasn't always true—my mother-
in-law worked as a volunteer, stuffing envelopes at first
and then becoming office manager and chief fundraiser,
with enough prestige, status, and honor for any five
people.

Many social agencies all over the country have training
programs for volunteers. It is one of the most outstand-
ing features of these agencies that so many staff members were once volunteers, greatly respected for their
genuine contributions. Typically, a sixty-seven-year-old
woman who had raised a large family of her own became
a foster parent and then adopted two of these children.
When all were grown she decided to return to school
and went to college. She was given college credit for
her volunteer work. She was later offered a paid job.

She turned it down, preferring to remain as an active volunteer while she continued her college education. Whatever she does with her life, she surely knows what being a volunteer can become.

This is not to suggest that every volunteer either needs or gets a salaried position. What it does mean is that if you choose carefully and really investigate all the resources in your community you can never once feel "like dirt." It's a two-way street; there are many places where volunteers are greatly respected and used in very important ways, but it means that they take their work seriously and don't just "dabble" in good works.

An important key to making a choice about becoming a volunteer is to choose a place that cares about you so much that it wants you to use all your potential gifts. There ought to be a training program as well; nothing could assure you more that you are being taken seriously. Of course it is equally important to choose an area of interest that truly excites you. A friend of mine said, "The best feeling is that you're scared to death—you know you are going to be really challenged."

If you can see yourself working as a volunteer, it is a time to make some very careful choices. Do you want to do something you know a lot about or fill some old dream of doing something entirely new? Do you know that the quality of your work need not be affected in any way, whether you are paid or not?

Feeling truly needed and making a genuine contribution to society in whatever area most interests you seems to me an honorable profession even if the "pay" is just carfare!

Our Assets
in the Job Market

I COMMENTED TO THE OWNER OF A SHOE STORE that I enjoyed being waited on by men of my own age or older since we understood each other; they never showed me shoes with high heels or shoes that would pinch my toes. The salesmen know without being told that I have reached the comfort-over-fashion stage of my life. The owner nodded agreement and said, "I have learned that one retired man, mature, experienced, responsible, is worth five young salesmen." He told me there was far less absenteeism, and even the younger women customers were relaxed about relating to a grandfather! (I did exhort him to extend his open-mindedness to older women as salesladies and he agreed.)

The point is that anyone who feels well enough and wants to work can—perhaps not at whatever exalted position he or she may have had before retirement, but surely at something that can be pleasurable. A woman I know was forcibly retired long before she felt ready to do so. She had had a most glamorous and prestigious job in television, and she was devastated. For months she remained paralyzed by depression, and if one suggested that she think about her interests and talents in a new way, she became angry. When she realized she could not live on her pension and Social Security, and would have to sell her co-op, she began to look around. She saw a sign in the window of an art-supply store, CLERK NEEDED, and, out of desperation, forced herself to go in and apply. Four months have gone by and she loves her job. She told me, "I realized that the main talent I used in my job had always been relating well to other people. Within a couple of weeks the artists who came in to the store were telling me their troubles, asking my advice, bringing me coffee—I'm having a ball!"

Another woman told me, "It isn't easy to relinquish your image of yourself as a dentist or a lawyer or a high-school English teacher, and I think this has kept me and some of my friends from having a full life."

Young parents are having a great deal of trouble finding good baby-sitters. The supply has dried up because teenagers are dating at an earlier age and seem to have less motivation to earn money. We are also, disgracefully, the only supposedly well-to-do country that does not offer adequate day-care facilities for working mothers. This is surely a field of work open to older men and women. Few things can keep us feeling younger than to spend some hours of each day with children. When I was a young mother I always sought grandmothers as baby-sitters because I knew they could take a temperature, see that medicine was given on time—but more important, were more likely to give a special kind of love, not too available, naturally, among young people with so much else on their minds. Rather than seeing baby-sitting as a menial job (as compared to office manager, department-store buyer, professor of mathematics, or restaurant owner) we ought to think about the fact that there is no more socially important function than helping to raise a generation of happy and decent citizens.

It is no accident that there are many gray-haired workers at McDonald's these days, or mighty healthy-looking lifeguards at a local YMCA pool who are over sixty-five, or in a thousand other jobs. It all may have started with a lack of available workers, but employers are more and more inclined to now look first for older workers because their assets are many and real.

Anyone who wants a job after the age of sixty and is able to work can get help. Private as well as public agencies working with older people can provide advice and resources. If the rocking chair is not where we are ready to sit, there are more and more alternatives open to us.

The No-Retirement Blues

WE HEAR PLENTY, THESE DAYS, ABOUT THE PEOPLE who dread the coming of retirement. It makes them feel old and they don't know what to do with their time; they worry about finances and they can't bear to give up the familiar role of worker.

Well, I'm here to tell you there are plenty of people who are *dying* to retire and are very depressed because they can't.

Take my dentist, for example. He became a dentist (and, of course, the best in the world since I still have several of my own teeth, a major miracle) when his father thought that was a good, safe profession. Later on he found out he loved to write. He found out he could build just about anything he wanted to. He's now sixty-six and he's taken up flying. Every Friday is the happiest day of the week. He wants to write more short stories. He's tired, but he can't afford to quit—never was a financier or an investor. If he could afford to retire, I would be up the creek with no teeth, but I know how he feels.

I'm sixty-seven; hardly a day goes by when I am not

in pain. I love to write and I hope not to give up *Newsday* until they fire me or I become comatose. I'd like to start writing plays and stories, but I know that would be for fun, not money, and I'd quit giving speeches if I could afford it, after forty-five years. Work keeps me stuck in New York when I want to get out of the cold and the heat. But we have to help support various indigent relatives, so I will probably never be able to just do what I want.

People who were never too crazy about their jobs look forward to retirement, as do people who know exactly what they'd like to do, at long last. People who have no idea what they will do with retirement dread it. And then there are the rest of us, who had this crazy idea that we would have enough money to quit working at sixty or sixty-five and could then pick up all the unfulfilled dreams of things we'd always longed to do. What about us?

I am ashamed to admit that I complain a lot. It gets me exactly nowhere. But I find that there are certain little things I can do that seem to help. I have a large sign, written in red crayon, over my desk: I WILL NEVER TRAVEL BY PLANE ALONE AND I WON'T GO ANYWHERE WITHOUT AT LEAST BUSINESS CLASS. I added that to my sign after a trip in which I had to walk about three and a half miles from a national to an international terminal carrying my bags because my flight had been canceled, and it took me nine hours to get home from a two-and-a-half-hour trip. In the process, I lost my aisle seat (I need to stretch my arthritic knees), and by the time I got home I had the worst sciatica and was bawling my head off. (Fortunately my husband was ready with a bowl of chicken soup.)

Another large red sign says: I WILL NEVER ENTERTAIN MORE THAN EIGHT PEOPLE AT DINNER. Reason: there were about twenty-five the day after Thanksgiving— only eleven the day before—and it took a week to be able to move again. My sign also says: NO MORE NIGHT MEETINGS (I'm ready for bed at nine) and NO MORE GOING TO CAPE COD IN THE WINTER (where my daughter lives and there has been a blizzard three Christmases in a row).

I don't have to add DO NOT SUFFER FOOLS GLADLY because I now practice that every day. I refuse to write other people's articles for them, I won't read typewritten manuscripts, I won't write letters of recommendation for total strangers, and I never answer hate mail.

I may not be able to do just as I please but in small ways I am retiring from the things I dislike the most. It helps. And taking one day off a week, to fly, keeps my dentist from having another heart attack.

Will I Ever Know
Who "Deep Throat" Is?

ONE THING REALLY BUGS ME ABOUT GETTING old, and it is I won't live long enough for certain mysteries to be solved. How can I stand not knowing who "Deep Throat" is, if he or she lives longer than I? How will I know who *really* killed John Kennedy? I know I won't live long enough to see this country come back to its senses—a world I once knew, when lots of things were far more important to most people than money and power; I may not even live long enough to see moral leaders, real heroes, come back into fashion.

Will I live long enough to see the world face up to the terrifying implications of "the greenhouse effect"? Will I live long enough for the subject of Elvis Presley to become a bore? Big things and little things—partly it's just ordinary curiosity, partly it's interesting mysteries, but I suppose the truth of the matter is that I am so discontented about so many things and want them to get better before I die.

Things like free day care for children; tuition for college based on the ability to pay; mandatory gun licenses as strictly enforced as car licenses; people voting for ideas, not television images; pornography and violence in movies and on TV voluntarily stopped because so many people care about children.

I would certainly like to live long enough to know that a cure has been found for AIDS. I know I won't live long enough for the world to decide that the single greatest danger to life on earth is overpopulation. I wonder if I'll live long enough to see Russia, China, and the United States as relaxed and friendly and free of paranoia as we are with our Canadian neighbors. I'm afraid I may live long enough to see the terrible bloodbath that seems inevitable in South Africa.

The thing is that we get so *attached* to life! Each of us has our own causes, our own dreams, our own curiosity about the future. Each of us knows it would have been nice if so many heroes of the past had only known how things finally turned out. Socrates, Joan of Arc, Pasteur—if only they could have lived long enough to find out they would become household names!

The simple truth is that mortality is the hardest reality human beings ever have to come to terms with. Each of us finds our own way to meet and accept that challenge—some through religious beliefs, some through the immortality of children and grandchildren, some through hoping their work will live on after them. It is natural to be curious about the future—to wish we knew some answers to current questions—but I try not to think about it all too much, to just live long enough to be useful and loving, and hope that somewhere along the way there will be some meaning in my having lived. That's all very well and a sensible philosophy, but I sure hope I make it to find out about "Deep Throat"!

We Are Not
Our Children's Children

A FRIEND SAYS, "CAN YOU IMAGINE? MY DAUGHTER
tells me I sleep too much and should get a part-time
job!" The mother in question is seventy-five, retired
about five years ago, and is having the time of her life
becoming a bum. She worked from the age of fifteen
and raised three children, alone after her husband died
twenty years ago. "I love my life," she said. "The more
I do nothing, the more I enjoy myself." She is exag-
gerating slightly; she still loves to cook, goes to concerts
and the theater once in a while, and visits and is visited
by old friends. She laughs and says, "When did our
children decide we are their children?"

An excellent question and one that any of us can relate
to if we have adult children. The truth is that they love
us, but it drives us wild when they want desperately to
take care of us! My husband knows he will have to eat
food he hates when we go to a restaurant with our daughter. She loves him so much that every time he picks
something he likes on the menu, we know she will say,
"That is not for someone with a heart condition." She's

undoubtedly right, but on occasion we feel competent to cheat a bit.

She happens to be extremely knowledgeable about nutrition and health in general, and has undoubtedly contributed a few years to our lives with the vitamin regimen she has us on, but sometimes when she's admonishing me, I feel as if I am once again five years old. Something in me doesn't want to be her child.

A widowed friend told me that her son had bought her a condominium in California, without even consulting her. He doesn't think she should live in a cold climate anymore, and she should live near him. She is over sixty-five to be sure, but she's still teaching one course at a university, and she managed on her own after a serious car accident. She said, "Imagine! Not asking!" I can imagine very well. I knew an elderly widow who lived in a somewhat decaying neighborhood. She had lived in the same apartment for forty years. She knew all her neighbors, the butcher, the shoe-repair man, the new owners of a small Spanish grocery on the corner, the pharmacist, whom she'd known for many years. Her children decided the neighborhood was dangerous and moved her to a residence for older people (i.e., a nursing home!) and she is miserable. "I would rather have died in my own apartment, no matter what," she said.

Until we become truly incapacitated, physically or mentally, we have to make it clear to our adult children that we want to remain autonomous for just as long as we possibly can; that we know they advise us or take us in hand, out of love, but (hopefully!) we allowed them to grow up and become independent and we would appreciate the same rights.

A friend told me that her third and fourth words as an infant (after "Mama" and "Dada") were "By myself!" Amen!

I tell my daughter that when I become ancient she can do with me what she will—but not yet. She says that when she knows I'm at death's door, she will put me in a soundproof room with records of all the musicals from the forties and fifties and give me nothing but candy, cake, cookies, and ice cream. I couldn't ask for a better kid than that.

Dealing With
the Retirement Blues

I MET A WOMAN WHO IS SIXTY-TWO YEARS OLD AND could now retire on an excellent pension. Her husband retired two years ago, and wants his wife to retire so they can both be free to travel and develop new interests—perhaps take some courses, be able to join a health club, and so on.

Millie couldn't explain why she was hesitant to retire. She told me she hated her job and had felt that way for twenty years. She had been struggling desperately to help people in trouble but the bureaucracy for which she worked had long since broken her spirit. "How can I retire," she asked me, "when I feel as if my life has been meaningless?"

I had heard many reasons why people hesitated to retire—fear of financial insecurity, loving one's work, no ideas or plans for things one might want to do, tedium, boredom—but I had never heard of someone unable to retire because of feelings of failure, of having wasted one's life. But the minute I heard the explanation I knew it was very likely to have been an unconscious feeling for many people who are unable to face that hidden agenda.

The more I thought about it the more it seemed to me that even if it might be very painful to retire on a note of triumph, it would be far more difficult to leave on a note of despair about one's life work.

Facing that sense of failure, not to have lived (and worked) as creatively as possible, need not mean a terrible ending. After acceptance and grief there can, of course, be a new beginning. If one's work was hateful and even useless, is that the end of the road? Quite the opposite. This is the moment for asking the question, "What kind of work would I do if I were starting all over?" By the nature of things we started working when we were very young and probably didn't know much about ourselves. By the time we are in our sixties, life has taught us more about who we are; we have unearthed wishes, dreams, and talents we didn't even suspect we had when we were in our twenties. What a great opportunity for reassessment now! I cannot think of any dream that cannot be fulfilled in some fashion in the later years. Maybe we now know we always wanted to become a buyer in a large department store; isn't there a small boutique or a dress shop in the neighborhood that needs a part-time salesperson? Maybe, after thirty years as a secretary, you know you should have become a nursery-school teacher. I cannot believe there is a day-care center anywhere in the country that doesn't need volunteers. Maybe you became a teacher or a lawyer, when what you wish you'd done was write musicals for the theater. Now is the chance to be a "gofer" for an off-Broadway or summer theater, or take courses in theater arts, or help kids put on plays in a community center. Dreams can't be rigid and inflexible, but with clever modifications and adjustments we can find activities that we've never allowed ourselves to try before.

I always thought that depression on retirement had to do most often with missing work. Now I think some of that depression may be the thought, "I never really lived." If that's the case it is never too late to start a new life, if we relinquish the past and use our imagination.

Things You Can Do Sitting Down

A SEVENTY-YEAR-OLD WOMAN I KNOW HAS HAD TO have two hip replacements within a year. Always very active, it had been torture for her to be confined to a wheelchair. For a while she seemed to be sunk in a deep depression, and no matter what anyone might suggest, her answer always was, "My life is over. I might as well be dead."

She had a right to grieve for the loss of her mobility. Her depression was to be expected and after a while she began to recover her natural optimism and energy. Eventually she was able to take her first steps back to an active and useful life. After about six months of feeling pretty miserable, a friend reminded her that she lived three blocks from an elementary school, that volunteer teachers were desperately needed, and that she'd been a terrific teacher for thirty years. She called the school, sent a letter about her background, and is now tutoring two children three afternoons a week. She has also had her apartment remodeled so that she can reach what she needs with greater convenience (higher toilet, lower shelves!) and says she is as busy as she wants to be.

When anyone asks her what she needs, she says she needs tapes of her favorite operas and piano concertos; she also says she needs stationery because she's now carrying on intensive correspondence with two nieces who don't have time to answer her letters too often, having young children and jobs, but who assure her that her letters are delightful and keep up their morale.

It is normal and necessary to mourn for the loss of our health or our active life. But mourning and self-pity are two different things. After acknowledging our grief, we need to realize that even having to spend part or the rest of our lives in a sitting position, all kinds of wonderful activities are still available to us.

Our fingers can, we have been told, do the walking through the Yellow Pages! One crippled woman of seventy-eight has made a list of all the telephone numbers of all the city and state agencies she might ever have to contact for help. She keeps this information in a file, and neighbors and friends know they can consult her about Meals on Wheels and home medical care, and anything else they need to find out about.

Bird-watching is a wonderful sitting-down activity. Even in a city apartment, a windowsill with birdseed can bring feathered companions. One woman wrote a charming book about the year she watched a family of pigeons and how involved she became in their lives! Meditation can also be a most rewarding sedentary activity, relaxing as well as stimulating. There are several good books on this subject (which can be gotten by telephoning a local bookstore, or asking a friend to go to the library for you).

Crocheting, knitting, or watching the good stuff on

television are other ways of entertaining oneself. There is also listening to the radio or tapes; reading is important, but what we sometimes forget is that writing can also be creative and fulfilling—writing about our childhood in order to give a family history to our grandchildren, writing about parents and grandparents, about trips, about how different life was when one was young. Taping stories about one's life can make a great contribution to the lives of young people.

One bedridden grandfather spends a great deal of his time making hand puppets for his grandchildren, who then perform puppet shows for him. A partially paralyzed woman paints birthday, Christmas, Easter, and Valentine cards, which are greatly enjoyed (and carefully saved) by her family and friends.

We need to ask ourselves what unfulfilled fantasies we may have had all our lives, that might possibly be fulfilled now, even sitting down. We will also improve our mental health greatly by trying to think of ways we can be of service, bring pleasure to others.

There's only one major catch in what we decide to do in order to continue having a full and rich life—and that is not to "lay our trip" on other people. Not to demand answers to the Valentines; not to expect others to answer all our letters; not to indulge in hurt feelings for a lack of thank-yous. Whatever we do should be because we want to fulfill our *own* needs and no one owes us anything. Those who are most bitter and demanding are also the loneliest; those who make the most of their lives and give with joy usually have more company than they want!

On Being
an Older Grandparent

I RECENTLY SPENT FOUR DAYS WITH MY EIGHT-YEAR-old granddaughter, who is a sheer delight—funny, interesting, charming; she's got it all. I needed two days in bed to recover. The problem has nothing to do with how much I love her, but with how old I am.

My mother gave birth to me when she was twenty-six. I was the same age when my daughter arrived. My grandmother was forty-eight when I was born. My mother was a grandmother at fifty-two. I was sixty-two when I became a grandma. Many of our adult daughters are now having a first child in their early forties. A friend of mine is about to become a first-time grandmother at seventy!

I have finally figured it out; no matter how much we want to have fun with grandchildren, we are *tired*. At twenty-two I could take care of a group of nursery-age children single-handedly, five days a week, from nine to five. The very thought of such a miracle makes me dizzy and weak now.

It's a serious problem. Every time I have to tell my

granddaughter that I'm too tired to run to catch a ball or read a seventh story, I feel guilty about making her see me as old. I don't want her to worry. I know there are grandparents who remain a match for not only grandchildren, but for tennis and jogging at ninety, but my personal research strongly suggests that this is a lucky minority. My friends and I bring each other chicken soup after a visit from the grandchildren. The problem is that if our children had continued to marry in their early twenties and had kids before they were thirty, we could have had a spectacular time with them. At our age all our grandchildren should be having high-school proms or starting college.

A woman I know who has concentrated on her career until forty-three is now pregnant. She told me she worries about how she will feel when she goes to a PTA meeting of the sixth grade and she's fifty-five years old. I worry about her parents, who will be eighty when called upon to baby-sit on the occasion of the PTA meeting!

All we can do is do all we can do—and no more. We need to find ways to be with grandchildren for shorter periods of time and to steer the play to more sedentary activities.

At one point my grandchild said, "Grandma, you're not *that* old! You still write books for kids!" What more can I expect of life?

Are You Playing Regularly?

I HAVEN'T GOT A GAMBLER'S BONE IN MY BODY, BUT there is one sure bet I'd make anytime—and that is that if you go to your doctor for any minor or major problem, you will be given prescriptions and instructions of various kinds but you will not be told that you must spend a certain amount of time *playing* every day.

Chances are that it takes you much longer to feel well because of this serious omission in your health-care program. We think play is for children only, and therein lies a major cause of many of our stresses and strains. Few medical procedures can do more to rouse the immune system to action than play. Psychologist Max Wertheimer once described an adult as a deteriorated child, and what I feel sure he had in mind was the fact that so many grownups lose touch with one of the most important ingredients of a full and happy life.

Play is doing almost anything that you don't have to do. It is doing something just for fun and not to make other people happy or to get rich or be a success. Play is adventure—welcoming the unexpected with delight.

It is exploring the inner world of one's own mind creatively—not painting by numbers, but splashing colors on paper, or pounding and shaping a piece of clay until something happens that pleases you. It is getting down to simple things.

My husband and I once had a rubber raft that we rowed around some marshes, bird-watching. People on great big yachts laughed at us but we saw envy in their eyes; we could take the air out of our raft, fold it up, and store it in a closet. They were spending so much money, they *had* to catch fish and have a good time. When it rained on a picnic when our daughter was young, we'd spread a tablecloth on the living-room floor. Child's play is not watching television and not playing cards and not even playing golf, pleasurable as those activities may be. All of these are organized activities or spectator sports. Child's play is singing little tunes in the shower, or smelling a flower, or watching a bird at a feeder, or taking a walk to collect leaves in the fall, or making believe you are someone else. Real play has no rules, no expectations, no responsibilities. It could be sitting under a tree or rocking in a hammock and not doing anything useful.

Children instinctively know that play is the best way to grow and learn. Even puppies know. Mud pies and sand castles. Taking apart a broken watch just to see what's inside. Daydreaming. A physician, weary with his day's work, flies kites; a man who sits at a desk all day paddles a canoe; a mother leaves her cooking and shopping and childraising to float lazily in a soapy tub. "I even play with the kids' rubber ducky," she says, "and when I begin to feel like a four-year-old I know I will feel refreshed for hours."

Somewhere inside each of us is a little child who wants to play, to be free, to imagine, to let go of the world of *Doing* and re-enter the world of just *Being*. A nice little nap in the afternoon, with an arm around a teddy bear, followed by cookies and milk, feels just as good at eighty as it did at three. Try it—the best medicine there is.

The Power of Pets

Wᴇɴ I ʜᴀᴅ ᴛᴏ ɢɪᴠᴇ ᴜᴘ ᴀ ᴄᴏᴜɴᴛʀʏ ᴄᴏᴛᴛᴀɢᴇ and live only in Manhattan, I suddenly got the most terrible urge to have a kitten. It was, I knew, the hunger to find some way to regain a closeness to nature, to be with something alive and growing now that I no longer had a garden or could be a bird-watcher.

Every time I see a kitten I can hardly bear not having one, but I travel too much and it wouldn't be fair to the animal.

At a recent conference I met Virginia Smithwick, community service representative of the Animal Shelter and Control Division of the Hempstead Town Department of General Services. That longwinded title has to do with the fact that Smithwick does "pet therapy" in nursing homes. Her working staff includes two dogs and two cats, and she makes monthly visits to each center. Sounds simple doesn't it? Ah, I can just hear you all saying it is NOT simple, it's fundamental!

Many years ago—much ahead of his time—my husband used to sneak pets into a hospital where his patients had terminal cancer. He got into a lot of trouble but, grudgingly, others had to agree that the patients who got to see their pets, even for a few minutes, seemed to live longer than expected.

In recent years, research studies have shown that pet therapy can lower blood pressure, help stroke victims recover more quickly, and play an important role in the handling of pain and depression.

All over the country more and more groups are developing programs in which the elderly can share some time with a pet. Apartment buildings, communities for older people, and nursing homes make a big mistake when they exclude pets from buildings. They miss one of the best resources to make older people healthier and happier.

I wish the kind of thing Smithwick does could be done all over the country. What is simple about this is that animals provide unconditional love; they don't care in the least if you have wrinkles or sit in a wheelchair or can't even remember your old address. All they want is to be loved in return.

Older people need touching, desperately, and don't get enough of it. Holding the warm body of a cat that is purring is a kind of special contact that begins to evaporate from our lives as we become widowed and children and grandchildren move far away and nobody has time for hugs.

The best people to demand this kind of experience are the old people themselves. It's just the sort of project that we can get under way, even if we are in bed. Write letters, make phone calls, bother the administrators, send petitions up and down the halls!

I want you to know the depth of my support: a big, friendly white dog who wanted to show me how much he loved me knocked me down, and now I have a badly bruised coccyx. I guess it's a good idea to stick to small pets.

Picture Buttons

I WAS STANDING AT THE CHECKOUT COUNTER IN A supermarket. In front of me was a very old woman having a great deal of trouble counting out her money. She was wrinkled and somewhat disheveled, and couldn't stand up straight. The young checkout girl was rude, impatient, intolerant, and uncaring. As I watched (and before I intervened) I suddenly thought to myself: Suppose this old woman had a button on her coat with a picture of herself at sixteen or twenty? Suppose beneath the picture there was a quotation from an English gravestone, "As You Are, So Once Was I; As I Am, So Will You Be"?

As I get older, and increasingly find it hard to recognize the old face I see in the mirror, I am more and more aware of how I must appear to younger people. And I am astonished and delighted when I come across a picture of myself as a young girl, for she seems more familiar to me than the way I look now.

Young people seldom have much patience with us; all they see is some old crock. All of us have had doors slammed in our faces, people pushing ahead of us when we need to get on a line at the post office or bank, younger people chasing ahead to get a seat on a bus. Mostly it's just thoughtlessness, but some of the time it is impatience, and distaste for older people.

I wish I knew someone who manufactured buttons and would take pictures we have of ourselves when we were young to put on them. But it wouldn't be very profitable, so maybe we should do this ourselves. I'm going to try it—buy a large button, put a picture on it with that quotation, and see what happens. Maybe some of you would like to try it with me. I'd love to hear what happens. It might be a service to younger people, caught up in the tensions and rush of modern daily living, who perhaps don't relate us to their own grandparents or perhaps don't give much thought to the natural cycles of life. I'm sure *I* didn't when I was young. In those days there weren't any supermarkets, life was less hectic, the old people I knew didn't go out very much; their adult children did their shopping for them. Buses were less crowded; life was slower-paced, quieter. I cannot recall ever even noticing older people out of doors. Now I wonder: when my grandmother came to give me her special, magical brand of TLC when I was sick, did she ever get pushed around on the subway? I know for sure she never worried about violent crime in the city . . . none of us did. (And it cost a nickel for her to make the trip.)

I think it would be good for our mental health to remind younger generations that we were once like them. And I think it would do them a world of good to be reminded that they share our humanity, our mortality—our aging. Next time I go downtown in Manhattan, I'm going to get myself a button, cover up whatever is on it, and create my own message. I can't decide between a sweet and sensitive picture of myself at twelve, or my wedding picture, or maybe a picture of me playing tennis or canoeing. It sure won't look much like me, today, but I want to celebrate the me I remember best.

P.S. When this column appeared in *Newsday*, I received a letter from Dr. Grace Cavanagh, the principal of a school for autistic children. She offered to have her children make the buttons I longed for! If you want one, send a dollar contribution to her at Public School 176, 850 Baychester Avenue, Bronx, New York 10475.

Keep Moving!

Wнеn I was a child I remember my parents teasing Aunt Renie and Uncle Isadore for taking a walk after dinner, no matter what the weather, wherever they happened to be. When I was a young mother I thought my neighbor was some kind of a nut because she fed her kids hot oatmeal and made them exercise every day for half an hour after school, while my daughter was allowed to watch much more television and had Twinkies for dessert. Neither my parents nor I had the last laugh; these people were all ahead of their time.

My husband, a research scientist, taught me long ago that when something new is discovered, it is a terrible letdown because once something is figured out it just seems so totally obvious. Now it is hard to believe that even a quarter of a century ago most of us, including the medical profession, which surely should have known better, didn't seem to understand that we are what we put into our bodies and what we do with our bodies. I wasn't really a terrible mother—but thirty-five years ago nobody had put anything into my head about exercise and nutrition. Now I know that my life depends on keeping moving—everywhere except to fancy restaurants, candy stores, and bakeries. Now it's run, don't walk, to the health-food store.

My father is ninety-three and it is clear he is too old to get the new connections. Nothing we say can convince him that the more he doesn't walk the less he will be able to walk. He just looks puzzled.

It is absolutely clear that most of us greatly underestimate the importance of keeping moving, no matter how old we are. In a survey of senior citizens, many said they got enough exercise doing housework or mowing the lawn. WRONG: what we all need is a sensible and carefully planned program which is not accidental and casual but which is guaranteed to keep the inner works well oiled and the heart beating properly. There are now dozens of studies showing that older people who exercise regularly are far less prone to fatigue and illness.

One of the great hazards of my life is that I sit at a typewriter so many hours a day. Those of us who have sedentary jobs or feel immobilized by some illness or physical handicap need to be most aware of all that we are in serious jeopardy unless we seek out professional advice about those activities and diets that can help us remain mentally and physically alert as long as is humanly possible. I think I'll go and take a long walk, right now, while I'm thinking about it!

When Children
and Grandchildren
Seek Psychotherapy

A READER WRITES: "I WISH YOU COULD EXPLAIN TO me why my daughter and son-in-law and their child are seeing a therapist. In the first place I feel guilty—did I do something wrong to my daughter? And in the second place my grandson isn't sick, he has some trouble learning and sometimes he seems overexcited. I admit he has a temper, but is that a reason for a shrink? If everyone with a temper had to go to a head doctor, there would be long lines around every office."

What a lucky grandma! Too bad she doesn't know it. When she was young people died of peritonitis because there wasn't any penicillin. People also suffered from psychological problems because nobody understood them or knew what to do about it. Now no child need die of a burst appendix, and hopefully more and more children will be helped with their unhappy feelings early enough so that they can fulfill their potential and feel worthwhile and self-confident when they grow up.

I feel sad that my mother felt so challenged, frightened, and guilty the first time I went to see a therapist.
What had she done wrong? I wish I had been able to
help her to see it was what she had done *right* that made
me want to examine my share of hangups, made me
want to grow, to live more fully. How I wish *she* could
have had the kind of help I was getting, when at four
her mother died and like any four-year-old she figured
it must have been her fault. She lived for seventy-eight
years with a terrible inner wound.

Never once in more than forty years in the field of
child psychology did I ever come across *anybody* who
wasn't carrying some evidence of crippling experiences
in childhood—some serious, some less so. Because it
takes so long for children to gain a sense of perspective
about events around them, they misunderstand: they
blame themselves for everything that goes wrong. It
never occurs to a young child that a parent or teacher
or grandparent could ever be wrong; obviously, if only
the child were good, bad things would never happen.
Every child ever born bears some of this burden of
confusion and misunderstanding, and what more of today's parents are trying to do is first make it clear to
children they are not responsible for family disasters
of any kind. And when children seem to be overwhelmed by inner obstacles, parents want to prevent
future unhappiness by solving the problems as early as
possible.

Psychotherapy, when it's good (and a therapist must
be chosen with as great care and research as a surgeon
or a lawyer), is simply a way of clearing up confusions,

encouraging a sense of self-worth, and is an avenue toward growing and changing that should be everyone's life task.

Grandma has nothing to feel guilty about. She's just terribly lucky that her daughter and son-in-law are using the emotional penicillin now available to us.

When It Becomes
a Matter of Changing —
or Dying

My friend Kate had a serious stroke last spring. For a few days she could not speak and was paralyzed on her left side. She was recovering when I went to see her, and with a solemn and terrified look in her eyes, she said, "Oh, Eda, this is a lesson I'll never forget. I'm going to change my life—you'll see." That was good news because Kate was ordinarily a wild woman! Never still for one minute, hostessing enormous parties with rarely fewer than fifty people. Her dinners usually offered turkey, a roast, and some fish; there were always at least eight vegetables (everything delicious, I might add) and three cakes and four or five pies. For three months she really took care of herself: dieted, walked, rested, did what the doctor told her to do. After about three more months she called and said she was having a birthday party for her husband. I asked if she was going to be sensible this time—something quiet, not too many people—and she assured me it would "just be family." I should have known right then and there. Kate has dozens and dozens of friends whom she considers her family. We arrived at her house and there was the old mob of yesteryear, Kate perspiring, never sitting down, shrieking with delight at each arrival, still cooking a more massive meal than ever before, all keyed up, just the way she'd always been: happy, loving, giving—and crazy! She had *not* learned that change in her lifestyle was essential to her future well-being.

I worried about her all the way home—and then it occurred to me that as a diabetic supposedly trying desperately to avoid insulin shots, I had had a second helping of sweet potatoes and a taste of the birthday cake. I know I have to change my lifestyle or face serious illness, and even though I have modified my life in many ways, I am still vulnerable to not changing. The lesson of Kate I hope will stay with me.

But I have had better role models to pay attention to. My husband, my dentist, and an army buddy (Second World War, that is!) of Larry's have all had heart problems in the last few years. They have all changed their lifestyles with great intelligence. They are more protective of their time, they have changed their diets, they exercise—and most important of all, they do not suffer fools gladly and can say "NO!" loudly and clearly when their new lifestyles are threatened by others.

Those of us who have tended toward inflexibility in our personalities and styles of living have a far harder time accepting the fact of aging and illness. We go on thinking we are immortal—just the way we thought in our thirties and forties. Denial is the name of the game.

When we left the party, I whispered to Kate, "I'm worried about you." She answered, "But Eda, I'm *happy*, I'm back to being *myself*!" I'm all for our continuing search for our truest identity, but sometimes a few modifications are in order, if we want to have the years to continue that search.

A Living Will

A FRIEND OF OURS HAS BEEN IN THE HOSPITAL FOR two months. There is no chance he will ever leave there alive. His immune system appears to be on a permanent sabbatical, and he is tortured by three or four catastrophic illnesses. His "quality of life" is almost total anguish. He can't eat, he is nauseous, he can't taste or smell, he can't walk or brush his teeth.

Until two years ago, when the first illness began, he was a giant of a human being: a man of enormous talent and success in his work; a loving father of four and grandfather of two; part of a creative marriage; a gardener of extraordinary skill. At fifty-five he rode a bicycle halfway across Europe. He was a gourmet cook and a great appreciator of the culinary skills of others. The quality and quantity of his friends were, and still are, a testament to a man who lived his life passionately and with great artistry.

How does one help this agonizing shadow of a man? How does one make the choice to let him die when he will leave such a big hole in the lives of so many? This may well be the most painful challenge we ever have to face and there are surely no simple answers.

For myself, I could not bear to hang on to life if I could not be *A Person*, if my identity as a human being were rapidly disappearing. But I would not want my daughter or anyone else put in the position of making the choice of letting me hang on or letting me go. Many of us feel this way and more and more people are thinking about attaching a Living Will to their other legal documents. Every state has different laws and regulations—some haven't even faced this issue yet. The circumstances must be carefully evaluated—it is not an issue about which we should make a hasty decision.

It is surely a matter too serious to handle on our own, and before making any decision I think we should talk to doctors and lawyers whom we trust. It is also something we ought to discuss with our children or anyone else who may be responsible in a crisis concerning our living or dying.

There are, thank goodness, more and more books and pamphlets to help us deal with this issue, new laws, and new experts. Any public library can help us find helpful information and guidance. It's a serious matter: the last important decision we may ever make.

Facing Up to Our Mortality

SOMEONE WROTE TO ME ASKING IF I WOULD WRITE about older people who deny their mortality. She had a special issue in mind when she wrote:

> My parents refuse to make wills. They are in their seventies, in good health, and in every way loving parents. They are devoted to their children and grandchildren. My brother and I have told them many times how hazardous it is not to have a will, because then one has no say about the disposition of one's possessions. We are also suggesting that they put their home in our names, so that if they ever suffered a catastrophic illness, they would not lose it in paying hospital or nursing home bills until they were penniless. We have tried to explain to my father that my mother would not get his entire estate (as he wishes) if he died without a will. He won't listen to us and my mother never argues with him. I think my father just cannot admit he will die someday. He even refuses to wear a seat belt although he and my mother were in a serious car accident last year.

Nobody who is happy to be alive wants to think about death. As a matter of fact, people who are unhappy don't want to think about it either, because with deep regrets about not having lived fully, one may cling even harder to denial of reality. In any case, it seems to me we have to force ourselves, if necessary, to deal with such matters as making a will, writing down in a legal way whether or not we want life-support systems to continue no matter how terminal an illness, and how we want valuable jewelry, paintings, antiques, and family memorabilia distributed. Without leaving clear and formalized instructions to the living, we can create chaos, both emotional and financial.

I know it isn't easy to think about dying. Since we have only one child, our wills are simple, but there is one thing I have not been able to face—and that is whether or not I want to destroy the early love letters my husband and I wrote to each other during our courtship. It isn't a fear of death exactly, but a fear of letting go of something precious and very personal. We need to make decisions about letters and diaries, and decide which is most important, privacy or a little immortality! It's a tough decision. I keep telling myself I'll have to read all the letters first and then decide. My father has shown me some of the letters he and my mother wrote to each other (on every possible occasion!) and I felt I was invading something very private, yet I hate to think of my father throwing them all away.

I suppose all one can say to a loving and concerned adult child who wants his or her parents to face their mortality is to let parents know how terribly hard it is, how much they are cherished and will always be re-membered, and how many choices they can make about the special things they value most. The money part is really the least important when you come right down to it; it's necessary, but will be easier to deal with if we give more attention to the things we cherish even more.

Asking a father who should have his father's gold watch-chain or asking a mother what should be done with a genuine eighteenth-century tea set may make it easier for them to make out a will. A sense of immor-tality has been established.

The Brain:
Use It
or Lose It

THE OTHER DAY I HAD OCCASION TO ASK MY
husband, "Where did you hug me?" It wasn't at all that
I wanted to place an historic marker at the spot—it was
that that must have been the place where I took off my
reading glasses (chain and all) to enjoy the experience
more fully, and I hadn't seen my glasses since.

Sometimes I don't see these glasses for hours at a time
only to discover they are hanging around my neck. This,
among similar embarrassing experiences, can make me
feel pretty old and foolish, but I am heartened by an
article in the *AARP News Bulletin* (September, 1987)
entitled "How We Age." The article is a report on a
meeting held in Washington, D.C., attended by scien-
tists and researchers working in the field of the aging
process.

The report is very encouraging. They concluded that
people in the oldest generation today are brighter and
more alert than their counterparts in previous gen-

erations. James C. Birren, retired dean of the Andrus Gerontology Center at the University of Southern California, reported on studies indicating that intellectual performance continues throughout one's lifetime. Physiological research on the brain supports this view. Brain cells, the experts say, *are stimulated by use*. Some physical decline attributed to aging is really due to disuse and is much more reversible than previously believed.

This report reminded me of one of the earliest studies on this subject. During the manpower shortage of World War II one enterprising psychologist rounded up a group of elderly people who were sitting around doing nothing and declining rapidly, and started a job-training program which eventually put most of the participants into wartime industries. Depression, passivity, helplessness, and the inability to communicate or to move around actively disappeared almost entirely. Feeling useful and needed and getting out of the rocking chair seemed to do wonders for the brain. John W. Rowe, director of the Division of Aging at Harvard Medical School, has reported that various physical abilities that do decrease with age can all be reversed to some degree simply by physical exercise. The theme seems to be, USE IT OR LOSE IT.

Surely better medical care and improved diet and sensible exercise have played an enormous part in the fact that today's seventy-year-olds are in far better shape than their predecessors. Robert Butler, of New York's Mount Sinai Hospital, said, "If you're productive you're healthy and if you are healthy you're likely to be more productive."

Good news from the experts, but the burden of proof is upon us all to find our own unique and special ways to be active and useful. I just heard about a ninety-one-year-old tennis player who has a martini with his breakfast; his partner at the tennis club is a meat, potatoes, and ice-cream man. That's not what the experts had in mind, but my philosophy is, "Whatever turns you on!" Just remember, these old guys are *playing tennis*. I know a ninety-two-year-old who knocks himself out finding chess partners so he can play almost every day—and it isn't easy because he beats the pants off almost every opponent. Exercise for the brain is just as important as any other kind.

I'm not sure I can do anything about losing my glasses four or five times a day, but I'm going out for a long walk, right now, and I'm going to have a fresh vegetable salad for lunch. And God knows I work hard. It couldn't hurt.

How to Be
a Better Grandparent

I WOULD BE VERY SURPRISED IF ANY OF US FELT WE had been perfect parents, even superior ones, even fair to middlin'. It is the most normal thing I can imagine to have misgivings or feelings of guilt and remorse. It is a sign of maturity and sound mental health to know that we are human and that we were bound to make mistakes we wish we hadn't.

The trouble with looking back is that we can't change the past. We can, hopefully, talk honestly and openly with our adult children, and even make amends—but the place where we can really have a second chance is with our grandchildren.

For all of my professional life my work has had to do with child development, child psychology, family counseling—until I got old! In the last five years I've had a growing awareness that my identity has shifted without my doing anything about it—and that I am not delighted by the implications! It has occurred to me that one way to keep my feet in both worlds is now to talk with grandparents the way I used to with parents.

We can do a better job as grandparents if we are willing to remember our earlier shortcomings and insist on being the beneficiaries of new and better information. For example, I think the very worst thing that has happened to our grandchildren is the way we now hurry them through childhood as if it were a waste of time: horrendous academic pressures, impossible expectations on the playing fields, a total disregard for the fact that if children skip any normal stage of development they can be emotionally crippled for life. The grandparent who gets my medal of honor today is the one who is totally uninterested in grades, reminiscing about how much simpler subjects were when we were children, and how nobody expected *our* parents to read until they were at least six or seven years old—if then. Since parents and teachers do quite enough (much too much) pushing, grandparents are needed for a sensible balance; children learn best when they are ready and when they are motivated by curiosity. We need to be aggressive advocates of that point of view.

The worst thing that was likely in our childhood and even in the lives of many of our children was denial or secrecy: not talking to children about real feelings, fears, or anger, not allowing children to participate in grief and mourning. The tendency of my generation of parents was too often the idea that if you didn't acknowledge a feeling, it would go away, and that we could protect children from pain. Now we know, beyond a shadow of doubt, that feelings can change and get better only when expressed and dealt with. A jealous child needs to know it is all right to talk about being jealous;

being afraid is normal, and so is anger. When a child loses someone he or she loves, the only way to come to terms with grief is to share it, express it. Grandparents who say things like "You can't hurt the baby, but it is all right for you not to like her when she seems to be taking so much of your mom's time" are pretty okay with me. Grandparents who say, "I don't really care if you're the best speller in your class—I just hope you will discover what wonderful things you can find in books" get a gold star. Grandparents who say, "I know how sad and frightened you feel; let's talk about it" are the ones I love, and finally, grandparents who say, "You are a beautiful and wonderful person, and I just want you to find out what you need to do that will make you happy" should feel they have more than made up for any errors in the past!

Don't Wait!

IRECENTLY HAD LUNCH WITH A WOMAN I HAVE NOT seen for forty years. My husband and I thought she and her husband were very angry at us because of some very bad behavior by a mutual relative. We let sleeping dogs lie. But, as Graham Greene once wrote in a play, "Sometimes sleeping dogs bark in the night." A few months ago we saw a notice in the newspaper that the husband of this woman had died. I had an impulse to write a letter of condolence. Shortly thereafter the widow called and said my letter had been so comforting—that she and her husband had never blamed us for the family problem, but thought *we* felt unfriendly. What a waste! And worst of all, her husband had died of a disease about which my husband knew a great deal—he might have been able to suggest resources they had not known about.

The widow and I both learned a lesson. When in doubt about any relationship—FIND OUT! The worst thing that can happen is to be rejected. At least then one knows one has tried.

From the vantage point of a long life, I have learned

at least one invaluable lesson: the things we regret the most are the things we did *not* do. Too often we are afraid to take a risk because we think we might fail. We don't go back to school—we might make idiots of ourselves; we don't take a trip that might be a great adventure—after all, suppose we got sick, far from home. We don't call a sick friend because we are afraid we might say the wrong thing—but we think of plenty of things we could have said (such as "I love you") after the friend has died.

When we fail, when we make a mistake, no matter how serious, it gives us a chance to learn, to grow, to make amends. When we don't take chances we end up half alive and miss out on what might have been great moments in our lives.

Holding grudges, being afraid to take action, or never taking risks are ways to die while we are still alive. Take a cake over to the neighbors you had a fight with about the noise of their conditioner two summers ago and haven't spoken to since! Just say, "Enough already!" Call a sister or a brother with whom you had an awful fight last Thanksgiving. Pull yourself together and go to the hospital where a former friend is dying. Just hold his or her hand and say, "You mean a lot to so many people." Make up with a spouse who lost his or her wallet and left you both eating bread and beans for a month! Go visit your grandchildren and let go of that silly pride which keeps you from asking for a wheelchair at the airport.

Life is getting shorter every day. What are we waiting for?

The Secret of a Happy Holiday

SEVERAL PSYCHIATRISTS HAVE TOLD ME THAT THERE are three days on which they dread seeing their patients: the day after Thanksgiving, the day after Christmas, and the day after Mother's Day! I really didn't need their observations—I knew all about post-holiday depression just from living a long time!

The problem has to do with expectations—with myths. Holidays are supposed to be blissful, untroubled, warm, and loving occasions during which all family members behave like angels. The people who are most depressed after a holiday are those who believe these lies! The people who have the best time are the ones who know that human frailty and imperfectibility know no calendars. A friend says, "I have finally accepted the fact that all during the turkey and homemade cranberry sauce that I slaved over, my two brothers are going to find some dumb thing to argue about." Another friend admits, "For a week ahead of time I prepare myself for the fact that Uncle Charlie is going to slurp his soup in a disgusting way." A grandmother admits, "The *second* happiest day is when all the children and grandchildren arrive!" (Just in case you have been unconscious for some time, her happiest moment is when they leave!) A woman once wrote me, "I have just thrown out the turkey leg that was stinking up my refrigerator, and vacuumed the house and paid the Christmas bills, and now, oh joy, oh rapture, I'm going to bed for three days and live on frozen dinners!"

The secret of a happy holiday is to see that your sense of humor is available at every single moment. You need it when your grandson spills gravy on your Persian rug; you need it when you are basting the ham with crushed pineapple, and your daughter announces that your granddaughter is waiting outside in the car because she's afraid you might have a heart attack when you see her purple hair. You have a choice of laughing about it or killing yourself when you see that the son and daughter you thought you had raised to care about each other are screaming at each other about which one knows more about what car to buy.

The thing is that any sensible person is *glad* to have a family who cares. The most civilized and civilizing institution ever invented is surely the family. At its very best it is the place where caring as much about others as about ourselves can happen. I'm no Scrooge; of course there is much joy in feeling part of our own special clan and celebrating our love for each other. But only if we don't demand the impossible; only if we take all our human frailties and allow them to be part of the festivities. Sure as shooting, your cousin Joe is going to want to know how much you paid for your house (it's none of his business) and your grandson, twelve, is going to tell you he's going steady, and the lemon pie is likely to curdle, and you will walk thirty miles back and forth from the kitchen to the dining room and your feet will hurt for a week—BUT as long as these unimportant details don't drive you crazy, there is a lot of good stuff going on for which we want to give thanks. Such as the sweater your granddaughter knit for you with one sleeve longer than the other, and the college-age grandson who gave you a bear hug after years of thinking that was beneath his dignity, and the joy of looking around the table and knowing that with all their faults these are the people you love the best. The best turkey stuffing has something sweet and something sour in it. That's life.

Children—
Our Most Precious Gifts

I CAN BE AS SENTIMENTAL AND MUSHY AS THE NEXT person; I can wax enthusiastic about the holly and the ivy; I am a passionate lover of Christmas trees in a secular sort of way since I know the Druids invented them and since they make the midst of winter bearable.

BUT NOT THIS YEAR!

In 1967 I published a book entitled *The Conspiracy Against Childhood.* What I wrote therein—twenty-two years ago—was that if we didn't begin to pay better attention to all of our children, we would someday reap a terrible harvest. First of all it seemed to me that too many people were having children they didn't want— people of all classes, races, and ethnic groups. I was an educator then, mostly working in early childhood education, and even within the limited area of my own work, I saw the beginnings of greed—the terrible urge for more and more *things.* I saw power as a new American "ethic." I saw discontented, restless women who didn't want to spend much time with their children; I saw mothers and fathers helplessly saying they couldn't communicate with their teenagers—and most of all I saw a culture that was trying to eliminate childhood by such academic pressures that children would be crippled for life. Too little playing with kids; too much focus on making money; too little attention; and too little of the right kind of discipline. Allowing kids to wander off into dangers because parents couldn't be bothered to set limits. I predicted a generation or two of kids who would be turned off from life, drawn to drugs—and even to suicide.

I saw all my awful predictions come true. Until this year, when suddenly everybody wants to talk to kids; everybody wants to watch kids; everybody wants to keep them from drugs and self-destruction. Until it became an out-and-out war against drugs, who the hell was talking to kids? Who was telling them they had to come home and pay attention to rules? Who was setting standards by *being there* with love and attention? Now we notice our children again because we have finally gotten the idea that maybe they could stop the drug war if we helped them to feel loved and wanted and appreciated— cared for seriously by genuine grownups who think caring about children is a serious business.

Whether you are Christian, Jewish, Moslem, agnostic, or whatever religious feelings or values you may have, I want you to *look* at pictures of the infant Jesus, at nativity scenes—not separated by different convictions, but all looking at the tiny baby, all thinking about what is more precious than gold, all thinking about holding children tenderly, talking to them seriously, and allowing them the fullness of childhood instead of force-feeding them with skills and knowledge they are not ready for. Let this midwinter festival belong to all of us as we take care of our children, not because they might use drugs but because we love them and know they are the most precious of all gifts.

The Shock
of Changing Roles

MY AGENT CALLED ME ONE DAY AND TOLD ME THAT a producer in California was interested in putting together a daytime television program. There would be a panel of experts and an audience to ask questions. I was delighted. I said, "Oh, great, I'll be able to talk about *children* again!" "No, Eda," the agent replied. "They want you to be the expert on old age."

What a blow to my identity! Nothing ever came of the program (it seldom does, I have learned over the years) but my state of shock remains. The thing is, you see, I was an "expert" on children and parenthood for over forty years, starting as a nursery-school teacher and working my way up to more than a dozen books about and for children. What happened? What did I do wrong?

I got old, that's what, and if any of us live long enough some of our most comfortable and enduring roles change. It's inevitable, but still confusing and even painful.

For eight years now, a very beautiful and charming

little girl has been calling me "Grandma." I still feel a slight shock and wonder who she is talking to. *I* can't be a grandmother—this is ridiculous. One "Grandma" of mine was a lady who couldn't speak a word of English, but let me know she loved me by handing me handkerchiefs full of candy and nuts; the other "Grandma" was that adorable person who came to play games with me when I was sick and brought me Nesselrode pudding, probably the greatest and most satisfying delicacy ever created and impossible to reproduce because now we know that three cups of heavy cream can raise cholesterol to the wrong level! My mother became "Grandma" to my daughter. But *me*? How could I possibly be old enough? And why do more people ask me to talk about getting old, now, when until just a few years ago they wanted my opinions on sibling rivalry and temper tantrums and toilet training?

Many years ago, when I was still too young to empathize fully, I led a discussion group in a senior citizens' center. People told me that the only way they knew who they were was as "Harry, the tailor," or "Rosalie, the mother," or "Marie, who sings beautifully." All had retired, all those roles were ended. Marie croaked a little just to emphasize her sense of loss. I was very upbeat; I told them they were still persons, and, of course, I was right but I didn't really appreciate their surprise and confusion.

What I am trying to learn to do is to keep ALL my roles, new and old, inside me, not as strangers or enemies but as allies and friends. Inside me there is surely a child I have worked hard to keep alive, to help me understand myself and other children.* Inside me is a scared teenager, a proud college graduate, a thrilled young bride, and an exhausted mother of an infant. Inside me too are the roles I still have—daughter, mother, sister, wife, writer. And now joining this club there is "Grandma," and writer about aging, and student of new aches and pains, and keeper of the flame of memory for those many I have loved and who have now died.

The shock of changing roles isn't so overwhelming if we keep careful track of all the other roles. When I hear "Grandma" I know that little girl can never see me as a little girl or a young woman, but *I* can remember. "Grandma" becomes everything I have ever been, with a new addition—a terrific role to be savored fully.

---

*I have written about this in a St. Martin's Press paperback, *In Search of Myself and Other Children* (1976).

The Passion
That Can Last Forever:
Growing

I WAS HAVING A BIRTHDAY LUNCH WITH A YOUNG
friend who was feeling uneasy about reaching forty. At
sixty-seven, I'm afraid I wasn't too sympathetic. I told
her that from my point of view she was ridiculously
young! She was not to be so easily dismissed. She said:
"No, honestly, I need help. The problem isn't age so
much, it's that I worry that I've stopped feeling passionate and I don't see how I can live without that."

Linda went on to say that she loves her husband very
much after sixteen years of marriage, and she would
never leave him or consider having an affair, but she
misses the passion of their first years together. She has
a job she enjoys—her work is "fun," but she isn't as
passionate about it as when she was in the first years of
doing it. She told me that she longed to feel profoundly
excited and that it almost never happened anymore.

I didn't know what to say; I think I said some foolish
and useless things about accepting change and the ad-

vantages of "the warm glow" as this replaced "the rocket flares." But when we parted I felt that I had failed Linda in some very important way—but even more, that I knew something I should have told her, but hadn't been able to put it into words.

The same evening my husband, Larry, told me about a woman he knew who was probably going to die of cancer, but had decided that for whatever time she had left, she wanted to go back to school and learn something she'd never studied before, but which had always interested her, and she wanted to see a therapist to try to figure out what had gone wrong in her relationship with her grown son and daughter.

Hearing about this brave lady, I knew immediately that what I should have told Linda was what I have known for at least the past forty years and couldn't believe I'd forgotten even for a moment: there *is* one passion that can last until one's last breath, and that is the passion for growing.

Linda's feeling of sadness suddenly seemed quite clear to me. I've known her for about ten years and in all that time she seems to have remained the same person: she has the same interests, reads the same kinds of books, sees the same people, and travels to places she's been before. There have been times when she was facing some personal crisis (such as whether she wanted to have a child before her "biological clock" ran out, and whether or not she should move to California from New York for a job), and I had suggested she might want to see a therapist to help her explore her needs and her choices, but she had always resisted the idea vehemently. "I don't want to be bothered with all that introspection," she'd said. It seemed clear to me, finally, that while Linda was charming and bright and warm-hearted, she was afraid of change.

How could I have forgotten to tell her about the one passion that can last a lifetime, when I had struggled so hard in my own life to learn to be brave enough to take risks, seek new adventures, explore the possibilities within myself? In the course of a marriage of forty-five years, Larry and I have changed so dramatically that were we to meet ourselves now, as we were in our early twenties, we would hardly recognize ourselves. In order to meet the challenges of our lives, we have both struggled endlessly to become more than we have been at any stage of our growth, and this process has become the necessary never-ending passion.

ABOUT THE AUTHOR

Eda LeShan, noted author of more than twenty books, including the bestselling *Oh, To Be Fifty Again, When Your Child Drives You Crazy, Learning to Say Goodbye,* and *In Search of Myself and Other Children,* holds a master's degree in child psychology, and has been an educator and family counselor for more than forty-five years. She writes a weekly syndicated column for *Newsday,* and regularly contributes articles on children and parenting to national magazines. For three years, Mrs. LeShan was moderator of the Emmy-nominated public television series "How Do Your Children Grow?" She lives in New York City with her husband, Lawrence LeShan.

More Books from Newmarket Press on Psychology, Inspiration, and Relationships

It's Better to Be Over the Hill Than Under It
Thoughts on Life Over Sixty
by Eda LeShan

Now in paperback with a new foreword by the author, insights and advice on such diverse topics as friendship, marriage, money, health, holidays, and grandparenting, written with warmth and humor by the *Newsday* columnist and family counselor. "This wise and entertaining book, rich in specific advice, will amuse and renew those on both sides of the generation gap."
—*Publishers Weekly*
(240 pages, paperback)

Share Jennifer James with a Friend:

You Know I Wouldn't Say This if I Didn't Love You
How to Defend Yourself Against Verbal Zaps and Zingers
by Jennifer James, Ph.D.

Excerpted in *Reader's Digest* and *New Woman*, James's book is filled with nitty-gritty advice for both the giver and getter of criticism, shows the difference between "constructive" criticism and encouragement, and will help readers defend themselves from—and laugh at—the absurd and harmful things we say to each other.
(144 pages, paperback, with illustrations)

Success is the Quality of Your Journey
by Jennifer James, Ph.D.

120 insights and ideas on subjects such as risk, solitude, aging, and relationships. Over 75,000 copies sold. "Filled with simplicity, clarity, beauty, and nuggets of truth."—Gerald Jampolsky, M.D., author of *Love Is Letting Go of Fear*
(144 pages, paperback)

Windows
by Jennifer James, Ph.D.

120 more inspirational and thought-provoking essays that bring an uncommon perspective to the topics of day-to-day living, including intimacy, risks, losing and winning, and travel (including the author's journey to Nepal), and much more.
(160 pages, paperback)

Ask for these titles at your local bookstore, or order from:

Newmarket Press
18 East 48th Street, New York, NY 10017.
(212) 832-3575   FAX (212) 832-3629

Please send me:

James, SUCCESS IS THE QUALITY OF YOUR JOURNEY
_____ $9.95 paperback (0-937858-66-8)
James, WINDOWS
_____ $9.95 paperback (1-55704-004-4)
James, YOU KNOW I WOULDN'T SAY THIS IF I DIDN'T LOVE YOU
_____ $10.95 paperback (1-55704-049-4)
LeShan, IT'S BETTER TO BE OVER THE HILL THAN UNDER IT
_____ $10.95 paperback (1-55704-102-4)
LeShan, IT'S BETTER TO BE OVER THE HILL THAN UNDER IT
_____ $18.95 hardcover (1-55704-071-0)

_____ Total books ordered

Subtotal: $ _____

*Plus shipping and handling: $ _____

NY residents add Sales Tax: $ _____

TOTAL AMOUNT: $ _____

For postage and handling add $2.00 for the first book, plus $1.00 for each additional book. Allow 4–6 weeks for delivery. Prices and availability subject to change.

I enclose check or money order payable to NEWMARKET PRESS in the amount of $ _____.

Name _____

Address _____

City/State/Zip _____

For quotes on quantity purchases, or for a copy of our catalog, please write or call Newmarket Press, 18 East 48th Street, New York, NY 10017. (212) 832-3575.

leshpb.7/91